THE COMING
OF THE FRIARS MINOR
TO ENGLAND & GERMANY

FIRST PAGE OF THOMAS OF ECCLESTON'S CHRONICLE IN
THE COTTON MS.

The Coming of
THE FRIARS MINOR
TO ENGLAND & GERMANY

Being the Chronicles of
BROTHER THOMAS *of* ECCLESTON
AND BROTHER JORDAN *of* GIANO

Translated from
The Critical Editions of A. G. LITTLE, M.A., F.B.A., &
H. BOEHMER

BY

E. GURNEY SALTER, LITT.D. *1875 -*

Author of " Franciscan Legends in Italian Art"
and " Nature in Italian Art"

1926
LONDON & TORONTO
J. M. DENT and SONS LTD.
NEW YORK: E. P. DUTTON and CO.

PRINTED IN GREAT BRITAIN

CONTENTS

v

LIST OF ILLUSTRATIONS

INTRODUCTION

I. NOTE ON THE TRANSLATION

THE translation of these two Chronicles has been undertaken in connection with the celebration of the seven-hundredth anniversary, in 1926, of the death of St. Francis in 1226. It is based on the critical editions of Professor A. G. Little and Dr. H. Boehmer respectively.[1] That of Jordan has not, it is believed, been previously translated into English at all.[2] Nor has any translation before this been made from a text of Eccleston based on all the MSS. The translation made by Father Cuthbert, O.S.F.C. (Sands & Co., 1909) is from an incomplete text, prior to the discovery of the Phillipps MS. The present translator has been much impressed by Father Cuthbert's skill in rendering some difficulties,

[1] Tractatus Fr. Thomae vulgo dicti de Eccleston *De Adventu Fratrum Minorum in Angliam*, and *Chronica Fr. Jordani* (Tomes VII. and VI. in Collection d'études et de documents sur l'histoire religieuse et littéraire du Moyen Age, 1909, 1908, Librairie Fischbacher, Paris).

[2] A translation projected in 1917 by the Rev. Fr. Auweiler, O.F.M., of Washington, U.S.A., seems not to have appeared. His preliminary Dissertation has been consulted and referred to in this book.

and has studiously refrained from any conscious borrowing of his successes. She has no first-hand knowledge of the MSS. The introductory section (iv) dealing with them is entirely taken from the critical texts, and much of the information in sections ii and iii and in the footnotes also. A few notes have been added by the translator, and for their accuracy, and that of the translation in general, she alone must be held responsible. Professor Little has been most kind in helping with difficult passages, and has supplied a few *corrigenda* in Eccleston in addition to those printed at the end of his edition. The occurrence or position of some passages varies in the different Eccleston MSS. The order in the text has been followed. Contemporary marginal additions to the Lamport-Cotton MS. (see p. xix) have been placed in square brackets. Where the identification of a minor place-name was uncertain, the most probable form has been given with a (?). The English form of foreign names is used, where it is familiar, e.g. Conrad, Cologne.

In translating quotations from the Vulgate, the Douay and Rheims version has been used.

Fratres has been rendered "Brethren," except when speaking of the whole Order, when "Friars Minor" has been employed, to correspond with

"Friars Preachers." "The place" (or "places") refers to the smaller Friaries; "Minister of England" (or "of Germany") to the English or German Franciscan Province.

The notes have been kept as few as possible. Page references to Eccleston and Jordan are to this book, unless otherwise stated.

The style in which the translation should be made has been a difficult problem,—how to give a mediæval flavour without overdoing it, and how to be exact without stiffness. It seemed allowable to translate the more picturesque or pious passages in rather different style from, e.g., the businesslike details of administration. The unwieldy sentences of both authors have been broken up and the irritating reiteration of such constructions as Eccleston's *ita . . . ut, licet . . . tamen*, has been minimised.

II. BROTHER THOMAS AND HIS CHRONICLE

Nothing is known of Thomas beyond what can be learnt from his Chronicle. He calls himself simply "Brother Thomas"; the addition of "of Eccleston" originates with Bale, the sixteenth-century compiler of an Index of English writers. Thomas tells us that he studied at Oxford, and was in the London convent during William of Nottingham's time as Minister (1240–54). As he says that he took twenty-six years to compile his Chronicle—which, from the mention of several events of 1257–8, and the omission of others later, e.g. the death of Adam Marsh in 1259, would seem to have been finished about 1258— he presumably entered the Order in 1232 or 1233. He does not mention that he held any office in it. Nothing is known as to his birthplace, or the date of his death. He knows less of the north of the Province than of the south, and seems to show a rather special interest in the East Anglian Brethren.

The Chronicle in places seems like a rough draft, notes and incidents being thrown in without method, probably with the intention of their being incorporated later. In spite of this, a very fair idea may be gained of the start and development of the Order in England in his day, and the information, so far as England is concerned, is reliable; in some instances it is confirmed by contemporary authorities. Eccleston is less accurate when dealing with the affairs of the Order abroad, and his account of the proceedings against Elias, and the Chapters General dealing with them, is confused and misleading. It is noteworthy that no mention is made of either the Second Order (the Poor Clares) or the Third in England.

Eccleston has little sense of proportion—of

what is trivial and what valuable. He retails gossip, visions and anecdotes with naïve eagerness, and dwells on anything that glorifies the English Province. His style is undistinguished; here and there he breaks out into a rhetorical passage. His Latin, though not a model, is less faulty than Jordan's. It has been suggested that his language in places shows evidence of a legal training. That Thomas himself, like Jordan, wholeheartedly admired men of learning is shown many times over, and one of the most striking features of his Chronicle, as Professor Little points out, is the union it exhibits of love of poverty and love of learning among the English Brethren.

Neither Thomas nor Jordan seems to have sympathised with the *zelanti*, or Spirituals. Their animosity against Elias was roused rather by his harsh and arbitrary rule. Both, however, without being extremists, note with approval instances of adherence to the bare poverty and the simplicity laid down by the Rule, and observed by the first Brethren. The characteristic Franciscan note of cheerfulness recurs in both Chronicles in many anecdotes, and in the praise of persons as *iocundus* and *hilaris*, but a note of Northern gloom sometimes creeps in, as in the opening line of Brother Henry of Burford's verses (see p. 44).

III. BROTHER JORDAN AND HIS CHRONICLE

With a few additions from Matthew Paris and Glassberger, to be mentioned below, the bulk of our information about Jordan is drawn from his Chronicle. But in this, in so far as his life after entering the Order is concerned, he is much more communicative than Brother Thomas. He also held positions of importance, which, so far as we know, the latter did not.

Jordan tells us that he came from Giano, in the Vale of Spoleto—a mountain village near Montefalco, which otherwise plays no part in the Franciscan story—and that he was in deacon's orders. According to Glassberger, he was received into the Order by Saint Francis himself. If so, it must have been not later than 1218 or early in 1219, as Francis went to the East in the summer of 1219. Jordan describes his journey in detail, and it is from that year that he begins to describe affairs in the Order minutely; he also mentions that he might have known personally the Brethren who were martyred in Morocco—and they went out in 1218. He was, at any rate, living as a friar in or near Assisi in 1220. He describes how he was made priest in 1223, but not his being made deacon, so that this had possibly taken place before he entered the Order. If so, he must have been born not later than 1195.

Jordan was present at the famous Chapter of Mats at the Portiuncula at Whitsuntide 1221. Here, as he tells us with engaging candour, he became reluctantly involved in the mission to Germany, from which martyrdom was fully expected. The early adventures of himself and his companions, his activities, and the posts he held in Germany, together with details of the successive Ministers and other leading Brethren of that Province, occupy the greater part of his Chronicle. It also relates his two visits to Italy, in 1230 and 1238.

Jordan is silent as to his life during the three years after 1238, but the gap is partly supplied by Matthew Paris, who, in his *Chronica Majora*, quotes three letters, of two of which he is in all probability, and of the third possibly, the author. The two first [1] were written from Prague in April and May 1241, and their language suggests an Italian writer; they describe the devastation wrought by the invading Tartars. Matthew Paris calls the author of the first "frater Jordanus Ordinis Minorum Vicarius provinciae Polemiae,"

[1] They are given by Boehmer, pp. 72–5.

and of the second "frater Jordanus viceminister Boemie et Polemie" (with another Brother). Now Bohemia and Poland had until 1239 formed part of the Franciscan Province of Saxony, so that Jordan, from his connection with Saxony, would very likely have been chosen to hold office there. But by the autumn of 1242 he was back in Saxony (see chaps. 71, 72).

After 1243 there is another and a longer silence. Nothing is known of Jordan till 1262, when, as an old man, he was commissioned to compile his memoirs (see Prologue). He probably died not long after, and is stated to have been buried at Magdeburg. This fact, and the date, cannot be established, as the Franciscan documents of Magdeburg have been lost.

The impression that we get of our annalist is a very pleasant one. He was evidently popular among his Brethren, a loyal comrade, and a successful administrator. He praises others generously, and his many stories are always good-natured, and often full of shrewd humour. One wonders if he *really* admired that Brother Nicholas who was so very " 'umble," or only tried to force himself to do so? The text almost suggests it: he was *ita confusus* (by the other's humility) *ut ipsum ferre uix posset!* The following description of

Jordan in Glassberger, very possibly supplied by his scribe, Brother Baldwin, calls him *iucundus corde*, and it is what we should have gathered: "A man of swarthy aspect, little in stature, jovial at heart, kindly, and ready for every good work, a man of great obedience, who reverenced in a Friar Minor no signs of holiness unless accompanied by obedience, or held them of any account." Like Eccleston, he is proud of his Order, and has an immense respect for learning in others. Jordan identifies himself with the country in which his work lay, and more especially with Saxony. The early days are told in most detail, and with evident enjoyment in recollection—even of the dire straits of hunger to which the little band were reduced on the Brenner. There seems to have been more language difficulty at first than in England, where the two English Richards acted as pioneers, and where Norman-French was a common ground for Brethren who had lived in France, and for the English. But the new-comers speedily gained popularity, adherents and benefactions in both countries.

Jordan is a more methodical relater than Eccleston, though sometimes he writes with an old man's garrulity and repetitions. He has disarmed criticism of his style by his opening apology for its

B

deficiencies. He latinises various Italian words, such as *sera* and *attediato*, but is not alone in that practice. In cases where his statements can be verified, he is usually found to be exact.[1] As with Eccleston, there are some noteworthy omissions, e.g. any detailed account of St. Elizabeth when writing about Thuringia, or of the later days of Cæsar of Speyer. The *affaire Elias* figures in Jordan as in Eccleston, our author taking an active part in the appeal against him. Here also it is his unconstitutional rule that is attacked—the "inordinate" Visitations, and the omitting to convene a Chapter General. Jordan seems to have had little sympathy with the *zelanti*, regarding them as failing in that obedience on which he set the highest value. One Minister he expressly praises as being *singularitatum persecutor* (p. 186).

IV. THE MANUSCRIPTS

(a) Eccleston

Professor Little's critical text is based on four MSS., of which the two first are fragmentary:

1. A MS. once at Lamport Hall, near Northampton, which is now lost; referred to as L.

---

[1] He admits uncertainty about a date, and makes two slips about place-names (cf. pp. 135, 143 *note* 2, 152, 181).

2. The Cotton Nero (A. ix.) MS. of the British Museum; referred to as C.

3. The Phillipps MS., at Thirlestaine House, Cheltenham; referred to as P.

4. The MS. (xvi. k. 4) of York Cathedral; referred to as E.

The discovery of the Phillipps MS. has proved that the fragmentary L. and fragmentary C. were originally part of the same MS., as P. copies L. in the early part and C. in the later. L. must therefore date from the latter part of the thirteenth century. It begins towards the end of chap. i. and finishes towards the end of chap. vi.

C. contains a number of other documents beside the *De Adventu*. The fragment of this begins with chap. ix. There are two styles of handwriting (not necessarily indicating two writers) of the latter half of the thirteenth century (probably not later than 1275), and many contemporary marginal notes.

P. is also a miscellany of contents. Its version of Eccleston is complete, and written throughout in one hand, of the early fourteenth century. It usually incorporates the marginal notes of L. and C. in the text, and adds certain notes of its own.

In E., the *De Adventu* comes at the end of a volume of varied contents. It is complete, save for a few omissions, and was probably written in the North of England in the first half of the fourteenth century. Internal evidence shows that it was copied neither from P. nor L.-C. There was probably some one original MS. from which all derived.

Brewer's edition of the *De Adventu* in vol. i. of *Monumenta Franciscana* (1858), in the Rolls Series, was based on C. and E. In 1882 Howlett, in vol. ii. of the same, edited the fragment of L., which had just been discovered, thus affording a better text for the portion contained in L. In 1885 a text was published by the Quaracchi Fathers in *Analecta Franciscana* (vol. i.), based on the above, and with no fresh examination of MSS. Father Cuthbert's translation is made from this. Another text, based on a fresh collation of C. and E., appeared in *Monumenta Germaniae, Scriptorum Tom. xxviii* (1888).

But none of these editions used P.

(*b*) *Jordan*

Dr. Boehmer's critical text is based on two MSS.:

1. That in the National Library, Berlin, originally at Königsberg; referred to as B.

2. That in the Landesbibliotek, Karlsruhe; referred to as K.

3. These MSS. have been collated with the texts of the late fifteenth-century Franciscan historians Komerowski and Glassberger, each incorporating large portions of Jordan's *Libellus* (see below). These are referred to as Kom. and G. respectively.

Jordan's Chronicle was well known till nearly the end of the fifteenth century, during which time it was regularly added to, thus being made an up-to-date Chronicle of the Province of Saxony. After this, it seems to have been lost to sight. Wadding, for instance, only knew it in Glassberger. The MS. in the Königsberg Archives was discovered by Professor Voigt, who made a copy of it in about 1830. An edition based on this copy (the MS. being temporarily supposed to have disappeared), and furnished with an introduction and notes, was published by his son in 1871.[1] In 1875 the MS. was transferred to Berlin, and a new and improved edition was then undertaken by the Fathers of the College of St. Bonaventura, Quaracchi, and published in *Analecta Franciscana* (vol. i.) in 1885. This edition contains various inaccuracies and, in reconstructing the text, the

[1] *Die Denkwürdigkeiten des Minoriten Jordanus von Giano* (*Abhandlungen* of the Royal Academy of Sciences, Saxony, vol. v. pp. 423–545).

editors did not have recourse to Glassberger or
Komerowski.

Dr. Boehmer was decided to publish his critical
text by the above facts and, more especially, by
his discovery of a fresh MS., that of Karlsruhe.

1. The Berlin MS. (Theol. lat. 196) consists of
150 leaves, of which folios 142–50*b* contain Jordan's
Chronicle, without a title. The writing is of the
second half of the fourteenth century. The copyist
was probably a German, as the German names are
so accurately given. He makes, however, mistakes
in other words, and in figures, and careless omissions. It seems certain, from several indications,
that this MS. is incomplete, and, indeed, it stops
at 1238, whereas we know that Jordan only began
to dictate his memoirs in 1262 (see Prologue).

2. The Karlsruhe MS. (357) of six leaves is also
a fragment. The handwriting is that of the fifteenth
century, and probably German. From internal
evidence, it appears to have come from the Franciscan Convent at Hildesheim. It begins towards
the end of chap. 58 of B., and carries on the account
from where B. stops (end of chap. 62), giving us
Jordan's résumé of affairs till 1262. It is to be
hoped that the missing portion of this MS. may
yet be discovered. It includes on its two final

folios a list of Franciscan Saints, Ministers and miracles, and also a catalogue of the Provincial Ministers of Saxony, and other details, between 1262 and 1360. This last would appear to be a continuation of Jordan's work collected in that Province. It will be found in Boehmer (pp. 63–7), under the title *Continuatio Saxonica*.

3. Indirect Sources: Komerowski and Glassberger.

The Berlin MS., of which Jordan's *Libellus* forms part, originally came, as an inscription on its first page shows, from the Franciscan Convent of Thorn, a German town in old Poland. It is, therefore, not surprising to find that it had been studied and used by the Polish chronicler John Komerowski. He took the Franciscan habit in 1494, and held several offices in the Order. He died in 1536, apparently at Warsaw. Komerowski was the author of several works, one of which, the *Tractatus Cronice Fratrum Minorum Observancie* (1512), frequently embodies sentences taken from Jordan, from MS. B., and copies almost word for word chaps. 64–7 and 70 from MS. K. He enlarged this *Tractatus* into a *Memoriale* [1] in 1534–5, and in this he borrows still more extensively from Jordan.

---

[1] The somewhat lengthy titles of both works are given in full in Boehmer, Introduction, p. xxii.

He would appear to have copied from some MS. now unknown, perhaps the original from which both B. and K. copied—a better and completer text than either of these as we have them.

Nicholas Glassberger was a native of Olmütz who became a Franciscan Observant in 1472, and composed his Chronicle at Nuremberg between 1506 and 1509, dying there at an unknown date. He had previously made several other compilations, e.g. one including the well-known *Chronicle of the Twenty-four Generals*, and his method with all was copying and compiling from various sources, altering here and there at pleasure. His work is, in consequence, untrustworthy. One of the documents he so treated was Jordan's *Libellus*; he quotes him by name, and reproduces passages, some of which are identical, and others nearly so, with those in the MSS. already described. There are, however, other passages for which there is no parallel in the text of these, and which suggest that he must have had a completer source, as, for example, in chap. 59. Glassberger mentions making extracts from the "writings of Brother Baldwin of Brunswick," whom it seems reasonable to identify with Jordan's scribe, the Brother Baldwin of Brandenburg of his Prologue. These "writings" were none other than the *Libellus* dictated by Jordan, but there is no reason to suppose they were Baldwin's original MS. The MS. Glassberger used was a different and better text than MSS. B., K., or Kom. In some instances, the additions would appear to be marginal notes added by a junior contemporary, such as those given in Boehmer, Introduction, pp. xxxvii, xxxviii. The personal description of Jordan (see p. xvii) may probably have been added by Baldwin himself. Glassberger evidently knew and used a text of the *Continuatio Saxonica*, this, too, better than that of K. He refers to one extending to 1488.

There may thus be said to be two versions of Jordan's Chronicle: (1) that represented by MSS. B., K., and Kom.; (2) that represented by Glassberger.

Dr. Boehmer bases his first sixty-two chapters on MS. B., and chapters 63–78 on MS. K., correcting both in places from Kom. and G. The translation follows his text, a few exceptions and variants, and the longer additions from G., being noted.

V. BROTHER ELIAS AND THE ORDER (1224–53)

It may be useful to give a sketch of affairs in the Order during the period covered by our two Chronicles, dealing with events described in them, and with that most enigmatic character in Franciscan history, Brother Elias.[1]

Even before the death of St. Francis, the direction of the Order had largely passed into the hands of its Cardinal Protector, Ugolino, and of Elias. Brother Peter of Catania had been made its first Vicar-General by Francis, when his own failing health compelled him to abdicate, but he died a few months later (March 1221). Francis then chose Brother Elias to succeed him — possibly under pressure from the Cardinal — and Jordan shows him presiding at the Chapter General of Pentecost 1221. Both Ugolino and Elias seem to have felt the need of more rigid organisation for the Order, of bringing it into closer conformity with others already established, and into closer dependence on the Apostolic See. For all this, a new Rule was seen to be necessary, less idealistic and more practical and compact than the first. How far this demand, and these modifications and formalisings, were a source of grief to the Founder can only be conjectured. If he condemned, if he was bewildered, humility and obedience kept him silent; it is but rarely that some poignant outcry reveals the conflict within. All held him in un-

---

[1] For a full account, see Lempp, *Frère Élie de Cortone* (Tome III. in the same series as Eccleston and Jordan).

bounded veneration, and a small band asked nothing better than to follow in the way he had first marked out. The majority of the Brethren, however, were probably of the same mind as Elias, and dreaded the imposition of impossible ideals in the new Rule. When, after some vicissitudes, it took shape in 1223, it was accordingly a compromise. It was confirmed by Honorius on 29 November of that year, and is referred to by Eccleston as *Regula bullata*.

In considering the character and rôle of Elias, we have to remember that our sources of information are mostly prejudiced against him. Some, such as the *Speculum Perfectionis*, and the *History of the Seven Tribulations* of Angelo da Clareno, are from the camp of his opponents, the "Spirituals" or *zelanti*; the *Fioretti*, compiled years after his death, gives an obviously exaggerated, bogy-man picture. Celano's first *Life* had been full of his praises; his second *Life*, and the *Legend of the Three Companions*, written during his disgrace, simply suppress his name, as does St. Bonaventura later. Elias was no Judas, but he had the official mind, and that was not the mind of Francis. He was an astute politician, ambitious for the Order, possibly for himself. But his rule became high-handed and tyrannical—the breaking of the

English seal (Eccleston, p. 94) was a typical act. And nothing can excuse his persecution of Brother Leo himself, Francis's most intimate friend, and of those who were likeminded with him, champions of the strict observance—of Cæsar of Speyer, for instance. Cæsar's imprisonment by his orders, and subsequent death at his jailer's hands, are not related by Jordan.

Elias will be for ever associated with the building of the great Church at Assisi; he began on it at once, after Saint Francis's death, to the gratification of the citizens, but to the disapproval of most of the Brethren, who realised how incongruous it was with the Founder's ideals. Jordan mentions the forced levies for this object. It was probably this general disapproval, combined with resentment at his treatment of Leo, that resulted in Elias's failure to secure re-election at the Chapter General of Pentecost 1227. Brother John Parenti was then elected; he was a pious but timid person, and Elias ignored him, and went on as before, supported by his old ally the Cardinal, now Pope Gregory IX.

The translation of the body of St. Francis to the new Church was arranged to take place at the Chapter General of April 1230, under the auspices of John Parenti, and crowds had assembled

for it. But, as Eccleston describes, no public cere-
mony took place, Elias having carried out a hasty
and secret burial two or three days previously.
His main motive was, quite probably, that which
he alleged, i.e. fear of the Perugians stealing the
precious relic, but some pique may well have
entered into it too. This high-handed measure was
disapproved by the Pope, but he nevertheless
gave his support to Elias when an appeal was
preferred against him, and, in September 1230,
he issued the Bull *Quo elongati*, which favoured
his party. John Parenti thus became discouraged,
and, at the Chapter General following (1232),
when the partisans of Elias made a demonstra-
tion to secure their patron's election, he meekly
gave way. Elias was accordingly elected, and his
election ratified by the Pope.

Eccleston's account of the above events (1230–2)
is improbable, and that of the *Speculum Vitae*
more convincing, as Lempp demonstrates (pp. 96–
100). The partisans of Elias, for instance, did
not intervene at the 1230 election, but at that
of 1232; John Parenti threw off his habit as a sign
of renunciation, not in order to win; Elias did
penance after his deposition in 1239, not between
1230 and 1232.

During his rule, from 1232 to 1239, Elias skil-

fully kept on good terms with both the Pope
and the Emperor Frederick. More surprisingly, he
retained the friendship of St. Clare. The Order
spread and increased, though some of the *zelanti*
practically separated themselves from it, retiring
to hermitages; others, as already said, found the
hand of Elias heavy upon them. Then general
dissatisfaction sprang up, for causes described by
both our Chroniclers. Elias summoned no Chapters
General[1]; he greatly increased the number of
Provincial Ministers, sending them arbitrarily
from one Province to another after short terms
of office; his manners were haughty, and he lived
in princely style. Finally, his unpopular Visitations of 1237 brought matters to a head. There
had been Visitors appointed as far back as 1229,
but none before with such minute and disturbing
instructions. Elias was appealed to, but with no
result, so it was decided to appeal directly to
the Pope.

Among the Brethren chosen for this purpose
were Jordan himself and Aymon of Faversham.
Bishop Grosseteste (in writing) and the Pope's
Penitentiary, Arnulph, supported the deputation,
but the Pope, to whom Elias also had appealed,

---

[1] He was not legally bound to do so, but it was contrary to all
precedent.

was reluctant to receive or hear them. The question of the Visitations was soon merged in a direct attack on Elias. But, according to the Rule, no Minister General could be deposed save by a Chapter General. So one was summoned at Rome for Pentecost 1239. Here attacks and defence, as Eccleston describes, were heard by the Pope, who became reluctantly convinced that he must give up his protégé. Elias was deposed, amid great jubilation, and Albert of Pisa elected in his place. The Chapter proceeded to frame a number of constitutions, largely aimed at limiting the powers of a Minister General.

The overthrow of Elias was not, as has been sometimes suggested, a triumph for the extremists or party of the strict observance; these gained little by it. The new exposition of the Rule that followed—drawn up by the *quattuor magistri*, of whom the famous doctor, Alexander Hales, was one—was not favourable to their views, while Papal Bulls and privileges still succeeded one another, to their distress.

Eccleston (though with faulty chronology) touches on some details of the fallen Minister's subsequent career — his ostentatious penitence, which might have produced a reaction in his

favour had not his refusal to obey the new
Minister General in one particular led to his
excommunication by the Pope; his transference
of allegiance to the Emperor Frederick, who
had himself been excommunicated early in
1239. The Emperor received him warmly, and
employed him as counsellor and confidential
envoy.

Meantime, Aymon of Faversham had been
elected Minister General at the 1242 Chapter,
and, after his death, Crescentius of Jesi, described
by Eccleston (p. 87), was chosen by the Chapter
General of Genoa in 1244 to succeed him. Here
Brother John of Kethene, Minister Provincial for
Ireland, vainly tried to bring about a reconciliation with Elias, who was living, with a small band
of followers, in a house of his own at Cortona.
A further attempt was made by John of Parma,
who was elected Minister General in 1247—the
"Spirituals" thus at last having one of their
number in the highest office. But Elias again
refused, apparently fearing that he might be
imprisoned. Shortly before Easter, in 1253, he
fell ill, and, after making his confession and being
reconciled to the Church, he was given Communion,
and died on 22 April.

John of Parma held office till 1257; Eccleston

alludes to his being released from office, but not to his being succeeded by Bonaventura; Bonaventura is the last Minister General mentioned by Jordan.

VI. THE ADMINISTRATION OF A FRANCISCAN PROVINCE

The method of administering the Provinces varied somewhat from time to time. It was more or less undetermined until the Chapters of 1239 and 1240, which framed it. Provincial relationship with the Order's headquarters was maintained by the sending of representatives to the Chapters General held every three years, and by the Visitors sent from these to the Provinces. These Chapters General, representative in constitution, were really the supreme power in the Order, as they settled all business sent up by the Provinces, and could criticise, elect and depose the Minister General.

In the Province itself, the Friaries were, at the time in question, grouped in Custodies. Each was a *domus*, or, if small, a "place" (*locus*). Over each Custody was a Custodian, who made by-laws, and visited all the Friaries of his group. Over the

c

whole Province was the Minister Provincial, who, as a rule, had usually served previously as, first, Guardian, and then Custodian. He summoned the Chapter Provincial, which was as important in provincial life as the Chapter General was in that of the whole Order. At first, it met at irregular intervals, but soon came to be an annual institution. In England, its exact constitution is not known.[1] But usually it was attended by all the Custodians, by the Friars of the locality in which it was held, and by representatives of all the other Friaries in the Province. These last, named *discreti*, were chosen at the daily, or frequently held, Chapter in each Friary. They stated grievances and made applications, etc. The aim was to keep the Chapter of a reasonable size, so that legislation might not be impeded. An inner body of four, known as *diffinitores* (*definitores*), decided what business should be brought before the Chapter. Resignations of the Custodians and Guardians were here considered, and new appointments made. The latter were nominally in the hands of the Minister Provincial, but he acted on the advice of the Chapter. He was himself criticised by it, and might be suspended, though

[1] See Professor Little's essay, "The Constitution of Provincial Chapters in the Minorite Order" (*Essays in Mediæval History* presented to T. F. Tout, Manchester, 1925).

not deposed, the cause of complaint being sent to the Minister General.

The powers of the Minister Provincial were thus limited, but he remained a very important person, representing the Order to the authorities in Church and State, and to the world; having the power of sending Friars where he would; regulating building and other affairs; admitting novices, and exercising general spiritual supervision. He attended the Chapters General of the Order, in company with a Custodian (representing *all* the Custodians, who had all originally attended) and two other provincial representatives; while he was out of the country he left a Vicar in his place.

The Minister General and these lesser officials were all known as *praelati*. The Minister General himself was supposed to visit all the Provinces. He could be criticised or deposed through the Chapter General only. The other Visitors were appointed from some other Province than that to which they were sent. After a Visitation, the Visitor would attend the next Chapter Provincial and make his report, consulting with the Minister Provincial and others. His scope was carefully confined. In extreme cases he might report to the Chapter General.

In addition, the Pope sometimes assigned a "Protector of the Order" to some particular Province.[1]

Many of these features are to be found in the pages of Eccleston and Jordan.

[1] The above information is drawn from J. Sever's admirable essay on *The English Franciscans under Henry III*. (Blackwell, 1915).

The administration of the Second and Third Orders is not described, as it does not appear in Eccleston or Jordan.

ON THE COMING
OF THE FRIARS MINOR
TO ENGLAND

The Grey Friars, Canterbury

ON THE COMING OF THE FRIARS MINOR TO ENGLAND

Here beginneth the Treatise concerning the coming of the Friars Minor to England, and their dispersion and multiplication therein.

HERE BEGINNETH THE PROLOGUE

TO his most beloved father, Brother Simon of Ashby, in the sweetness of Our Lord and Saviour Jesus Christ, Thomas, his Brother, wisheth the consolation of the Holy Spirit.

Forasmuch as the just man ought to judge his own life by the examples of many, since examples are often better incentives than the precepts of reason, and in order that you may have examples from among your own people wherewith to strengthen your most dearly loved sons; in order, moreover, that those same sons—who, for the sake of following our Order and condition, have yielded up so many and so great advantages, yea, and their own selves with them—should, when they read or hear the marvels of other Orders, possess matter no less edifying in their own, and should pay thanks unfailing to Him Who called them, sweet Jesus—behold, most beloved father in sweet Jesus, I set before you what I have put together, what it is my joy to have acquired throughout twenty-six years from my dearest teachers and fellow-pupils. Wherefore, to the honour of Him in Whom God the Father is well-pleased, Jesus Christ, our most sweet Lord God, I send you this little work.

[TABLE OF CHAPTERS]

[1] In the heading of chap. xv. "special" is substituted for "spiritual."

5

[CHAPTER I]

OF THE FIRST COMING OF THE FRIARS MINOR
TO ENGLAND

IN the year of Our Lord 1224, in the time of
the lord Pope Honorius, in the same year, to
wit, as that in which he confirmed the Rule of
Blessed Francis; in the eighth year of the reign
of the lord King Henry, son of John, on the third
day in the week after the Feast of the Nativity
of the Blessed Virgin,[1] which in that year fell on
a Sunday, the Friars Minor first arrived in England, at Dover, being four clerks and five laymen.

The clerks were these: first, Brother Agnellus of
Pisa, in orders a deacon, in age about thirty, who
at the last Chapter General had been designated
by Blessed Francis as Minister Provincial for
England; he had been Custodian at Paris, and
had borne himself there so discreetly as to win
the highest favour among the Brethren and
layfolk alike by reason of his renowned holiness.

---

[1] 8 September, i.e. they arrived on Tuesday, 10th. For *feria
tertia*, cf. p. 138, note 2. The Rule was confirmed on 29 November,
1223. Eccleston probably makes the year start with Advent.

The second was Brother Richard of Ingworth,[1] an Englishman by birth, a priest and preacher, and more elderly; he was the first member of the Order who preached publicly north of the Alps. In course of time, under Brother John Parenti [2] of happy memory, he was sent to Ireland to be Minister Provincial. He had been Brother Agnellus' Vicar whilst Agnellus himself went to the Chapter General in which the Translation of the body of Saint Francis was carried out, and had set a notable example of exceeding holiness. When he had fulfilled his faithful ministry, well-pleasing to God, he was relieved from all office among the Brethren at the Chapter General [3] under Brother Albert of happy memory, and, fired by zeal for the faith, set out for Syria and there, making a good death, fell on sleep.

The third was Brother Richard of Devon, also an Englishman by birth, in orders an acolyte, in age a youth; he left us many examples of long-suffering and obedience. For after he had travelled through divers Provinces, on holy obedience, albeit often during eleven years worn out by quartan fevers, he abode uninterruptedly at the place of Romney.[4]

---

[1] In Norfolk.   [2] Cf. p. xxviii.   [3] In 1239.
[4] The smaller Franciscan Houses were called "places" (*loca*). Cf. p. xxxiii.

The fourth was Brother William of Ashby,[1] still a novice, wearing the hood of a probationer, like these others English by birth, youthful in age, and in his standing. He for a long time persevered in praiseworthy fashion in various offices, the spirit of Jesus Christ aiding him, and showed us examples of humility and poverty, love and gentleness, of obedience and patience and all perfection. For when Brother Gregory, Minister in France, asked of him if he willed to go to England, he replied that he did not know. And when the Minister marvelled at this reply, Brother William said at last that the reason he did not know what he willed was that his will was not his own but the Minister's. Wherefore he willed whatsoever the Minister willed him to will. Brother William of Nottingham testified of him that he was perfect in obedience, for when he offered him the choice of the place where he would live, he said that that place best pleased him which it pleased the Brother to appoint for him.

[And because he was specially gifted with charm and of a most prepossessing gentleness, he called forth the goodwill of many layfolk towards the Order. Moreover, he brought into the way of salvation many meet persons of divers positions,

[1] There were several places of this name in England.

ages, and ranks, and in many ways he gave convincing proof that sweet Jesus knew how to do marvellous things and by locusts to vanquish giants.[1]]

[At a time of fleshly temptation, he, in his zeal for chastity, mutilated himself. After which he sought the Pope, who, though severely reproving him, granted him a dispensation so that he might celebrate the Divine Offices. This same William after many years died peacefully in London.]

Now the laymen were these: first, Brother Henry of Treviso, a Lombard by birth, who by reason of his saintliness and notable sagacity was afterward made Guardian at London. When he had fulfilled the course of his labour in England, the number of the Brethren having already increased, he returned to his own country. The second was Brother Lawrence of Beauvais, who at first worked in manual labour, as the Rule enjoined.[2] After he returned to Blessed Francis, he earned the privilege of seeing him often and being consoled by converse with him; finally, the holy Father most generously bestowed on him his own tunic, and sent him back to England gladdened by his most sweet blessing. This Lawrence, after many toils and, as I think, through

[1] An allusion to Num. xiii. 33 (A.V. grasshoppers).
[2] *Regula Prima*, cap. 7: "Let those Brethren who know how to work, do so, and practise the trade that they have learnt."

the merits of that same Father, reached the haven of quiet, London, where he now lies sick beyond recovery, and awaits the end of his long labours. The third was Brother William of Florence who, after the Brethren had been received, returned speedily to France. The fourth was Brother Melioratus. The fifth was Brother James, from the other side of the Alps, still a novice, wearing a probationer's hood.

These nine were conveyed across to England in loving wise by the monks of Fécamp, and by them courteously sustained in their need. When they reached Canterbury, they abode for two days at the Priory of the Holy Trinity.[1] Thence without delay four of them went on to London, to wit, Brother Richard of Ingworth, Brother Richard of Devon, Brother Henry and Brother Melioratus. The other five betook themselves to a priests'[2] hostel, where they remained until they had found a place for themselves. For, shortly after, a small room under a schoolhouse was granted them, where by day they sat uninterruptedly as though shut in. But when the scholars had returned home at evening, they came into the schoolhouse in which they had sat

---

[1] i.e. Christ Church, the Cathedral.

[2] The Poor Priests' Hospital, called also St. Mary's. The old Grammar School (see next sentence) was under the control of the monks of Christ Church.

and there made them a fire and sat beside it.
And sometimes they set on the fire a little pot
containing dregs of beer, when it was time to
drink at the evening collation, and they put a
saucer in the pot and drank in turn, and one by
one they spake some word of edification. And one
who was their associate in this unfeigned simplicity and holy poverty, and merited to be a
partaker thereof, bore witness that their drink
was sometimes so thick that, when the saucers had
to be heated, they poured water upon it, and thus
drank it with joy. The like often befell at Salisbury
too, where the Brethren drank these dregs round the
fire in the kitchen at the evening collation, with
such light-heartedness and gladness that he counted
himself happy who could snatch them in a friendly
way from another. Old Brother Martin congratu-
lated himself on having done this very thing at
Shrewsbury, when the Brethren first came to that
place; it was he who inaugurated that place.

In those days the Brethren so strictly refrained
from contracting debts that they scarcely con-
sented to borrow money for their most urgent
needs. Now it befell that Brother Agnellus,
with Brother Solomon,[1] the Guardian of London,
wished to audit the reckoning of the Brethren

[1] Cf. p. 17.

there—how much, to wit, they had spent in one term of the year. When he learnt that they had proceeded so lavishly (albeit the sustenance of the Brethren was frugal enough) he threw down all the tallies and parchments and, smiting himself in the face, exclaimed: *Ay me cattivo!* [1] and would never thereafter audit their reckoning.

Again, it chanced that two Brethren came to a certain place of the Brethren in sore trouble, and, as there was no beer in the house, the Guardian, by the advice of the elder Brethren, caused a flagon of beer to be taken in on credit, but in such wise that the Brethren of the house who were with their guests did not drink therefrom, but pretended to drink, for charity's sake.

[Up to the time of the formation of the Order,[2] the Brethren were wont to make a collation every day and, those who wished it, to drink in common, and to hold a Chapter every day. Nor were they limited in receiving divers dishes, or wine, except that they did not allow food to be offered them save on three days each week in most places. In that same convent of London, at the time when Brother William of pious memory was Minister, and Brother Hugh Guardian, I saw the Brethren

---

[1] *Ay me captivum!* The exclamation would be in Italian, probably as rendered above (perhaps *Oimè!*). It practically means "Alas!"
[2] It is not clear what date is meant.

drinking beer that was so sour that some preferred to drink water, and eating the bread which is commonly called *torta*. Indeed, when bread was lacking, I have for a considerable time eaten sub-stitutes,[1] in the presence of the Minister aforesaid, and of guests in the guest-house.]

---

[1] *Alia.* An emendation of *alicam* (=spelt) has been proposed.

D

CHAPTER II

OF THE FIRST GROUPING OF THE BRETHREN

NOW the four Brethren already named, when they reached London, betook them to the Friars Preachers,[1] and were by them graciously received; with them they abode for fifteen days, eating and drinking what was set before them, as though most entirely members of their house. After this they hired a house for themselves in Cornhill, and made cells for themselves in it, stopping up the holes in the cells with grasses. And they abode there in that simple state until the following summer, with no chapel, for they had not yet been granted the privilege of setting up altars and celebrating the Divine Offices in their places.

And without delay, before the Feast of All Saints,[2] and even before Brother Agnellus came to London, Brother Richard of Ingworth and Brother Richard of Devon set forth for Oxford,

[1] The Dominicans, who had settled in London in 1221, on the present site of Lincoln's Inn.
[2] 1 November.

and there in the same most friendly manner were
received by the Friars Preachers; they ate in their
refectory and slept in their dormitory like members
of their house for eight days. Thereafter they hired
a house for themselves in the parish of Saint Ebbe's,
and there they remained, with no chapel, until the
following summer. There sweet Jesus sowed a grain
of mustard-seed that afterward became greater
than all herbs. Thence Brother Richard of Ingworth and Brother Richard of Devon set forth to
Northampton, and were received in the Hospital.
Afterward they hired a house for themselves in
the parish of Saint Giles, where the first Guardian
was Brother Peter the Spaniard, he who wore an
iron corselet next his skin, and gave many other
examples of perfection.

The first Guardian at Oxford was Brother
William of Ashby, until then a novice; howbeit,
the habit of his profession was granted him. The
first Guardian at Cambridge was Brother Thomas
of Spain; the first at Lincoln,[1] Brother Henry
Misericord, a layman: [under whom Brother John
of Yarmouth was a member of the house, a man
of great holiness, who afterward died at Nottingham, and is buried among the Canons [2] at Selford.]

[1] The dates of the founding of the Cambridge and Lincoln friaries
are not known; both were probably before 1230.
[2] i.e. Augustinians.

[Sir John Travers [1] first received the Brethren in Cornhill, and hired a house for them, and a certain Lombard, a layman, Henry [2] by name, was made Guardian; he then for the first time learnt to read, by night, in the Church of Saint Peter, Cornhill. Afterward he was made Vicar of the English Province while Brother Agnellus was absent at the Chapter General. He had, however, as Coadjutor in the Vicariate, Brother Richard of Ingworth. But he did not support such a high state of happiness unto the end, but rather grew luxurious in these honours, and, estranged from his true self, apostatised from the Order in pitiable fashion.]

[It is worthy of record that in the second year of the administration of Brother Peter, the fifth Minister in England, in the thirty-second year, to wit, from the coming of the Brethren to England,[3] the Brethren living in England, in forty-nine places, were numbered at twelve hundred and forty-two.]

[1] A Sheriff of London from 1223 to 1225.
[2] Cf. p. 9.
[3] i.e. in 1256. This paragraph, inserted here by E., and at the end of chap. iii. by P., would follow more naturally after chap. iv.

CHAPTER III

OF THE RECEPTION OF NOVICES

NOW when the Brethren who first came to England had separated, and gone forth to divers places, certain men, whom the spirit of Jesus impelled thereto, came seeking admission to the Order. Of these the first to be received was a youth of good disposition and comely to look on, the much-renowned Brother Solomon. He was wont to tell me how, while still a novice, he was made procurator,[1] and came to his sister's house to beg for alms. She, as she brought him bread, turned her face from him, saying: "Cursed be the hour wherein I ever saw thee"; he, for his part, took the bread, rejoicing, and went his way.

Brother Solomon kept the rule of utterest poverty so strictly before him that, though he would at times carry in his hood meal, or salt, or a few poor little figs, for the sake of some sick brother, and wood for the fire under his arm, he

---

[1] The procurators were laymen entrusted with the temporal affairs of the community.

yet most carefully refrained from accepting or keeping anything that was beyond the limits of absolute necessity. Whence it once befell that he suffered so intensely from cold that he thought he would die then and there. Then, as the Brethren had nothing wherewith to warm themselves, holy charity taught them a pious remedy. All the Brethren crowded round him, and warmed him by huddling against him in the way that pigs do.

Now when Solomon was to be advanced to the order of acolyte, he was sent to the venerable Father of holy memory, Archbishop Stephen,[1] and presented to him by a certain older Brother. The Archbishop received him most favourably, and advanced him to the desired order in these words: "Let Brother Solomon of the Order of the Apostles be admitted." This I have reported that it may be observed in what respect wise men held the early simplicity of the Brethren. When they had eaten at the Archbishop's table, they returned to Canterbury barefoot in the snow, which lay very deep and terrifying to all beholders. As a result, gout afflicted him in one foot, by reason of which he lay sick in London for two years, nor could he scarce ever move about unless he were carried. In this sickness he merited to be visited by Brother

[1] Stephen Langton, *d*. 1228.

Jordan of holy memory, Master-General of the Order of Friars Preachers, who said to him: "Brother, be not ashamed, although the Father of Our Lord Jesus Christ draw thee to Him by the foot." Now after that he had lain so long a time in his cell, where he could not hear Mass—for the Brethren did not celebrate in the friary, but went to the parish church to hear the Divine Offices and to celebrate—his disease grew so desperate that, by the advice of the surgeons, it was thought necessary to amputate the foot. When the axe was approached, and the foot uncovered, a sort of matter was discharged which gave some hope; wherefore that painful verdict was postponed at that time. Meanwhile Brother Solomon conceived a sure hope that if he were taken to the shrine of St. Eloi [1] he might recover his foot and his health. When Brother Agnellus arrived there, he ordered that he should be taken to the shrine of St. Eloi oversea without delay, and in whatever manner might most conveniently be compassed. This was done, nor did his confidence deceive him; nay, indeed, he afterward so much recovered that he could walk without a stick, and could celebrate Masses, and became Guardian in London and Confessor General to the whole city.

[1] At Noyon.

Nevertheless, because he had implored Jesu most sweet to cleanse him from his sins in this present life, He sent upon him a gout [1] which brake the spine of his back so that he became humpbacked and crooked; He sent upon him fever and dropsy, and frequent bleeding from piles, until his death. And at the last, on the day before he departed to sweet Jesus, He sent upon him such pain of heart, the cause whereof he knew not, that all his sufferings before it he held as naught in comparison with that anguish. Therefore, calling to him three Brothers who were his more intimate friends, he showed them the conflict of his soul, and earnestly besought them that they should be instant in prayer for his condition. While they, accordingly, were continuing in prayer with one mind, there appeared unto him Jesus most sweet, accompanied by Blessed Peter the Apostle, standing by his bed and looking upon him. Brother Solomon, at once recognising the Saviour, cried: "Have mercy upon me, Lord, have mercy upon me!" And the Lord Jesus replied: "Because thou hast always prayed Me that in this present life I would fully afflict and cleanse thee, I have sent thee the pain thou now endurest, and in especial because thou hast left thy first love, and hast not

---

[1] *Gutta.* (?) Lumbago.

shown, as befitted thy vocation, meet fruits of penance; also, thou hast too much spared the rich in laying penances upon them." And Blessed Peter added: "Know, moreover, that thou hast erred grievously in judging Brother John of Chichester, who lately deceased. And now pray God that He may give thee such an end as that Brother had." And Brother Solomon cried aloud, and said: "Have mercy upon me, sweetest Lord, have mercy upon me, sweet Jesu!" He, smiling, looked upon him so benignly that all his former agony ceased, and he was filled with spiritual rejoicing, and conceived a most sure hope of his own salvation. He immediately called the Brethren, and related what he had seen, whereby they were no little comforted.

[It is worthy of record that, while the Brethren were in their place in Cornhill, the devil appeared in visible form and said to Brother Gilbert of Wyke as he was sitting alone: "Dost thou think to have escaped me? Lo, this shalt thou have yet," and he threw over him a handful of lice, and vanished.]

The second Brother who was received by Brother Agnellus was Brother William of London, who was at one time dumb, but at Barking, by the merits of Saint Ethelburga, as he told me, recovered his speech. While he was a member of the household of the Lord Justiciar of England, Hubert de Burgh, he, albeit a layman and a scholar,[1] as was thought, was also a famous tailor. He received the habit in London before the Brethren had lands or a chapel there.

The third was Brother Jocelyn of Cornhill, a youth of excellent disposition, of noble birth, and delicate upbringing, a Londoner by birth and a clerk. After enduring many toils in London, he set forth to Spain to dwell there, and there he died in peace.

The fourth was brother John, a clerk, a youth of about eighteen years, of good disposition and excellent conduct. He quickly ran his earthly course, and departed to Our Lord Jesus Christ. It was he who persuaded Sir Philip, a priest, when he was suffering excessively from his teeth, to send bread and beer to the Friars Minor, promising that the Lord Jesus would cure him. Thereafter they both speedily dedicated themselves and entered the Order of Friars Minor.

The fifth was this same Brother Philip, a Londoner by birth, in priest's orders, who was afterwards made Guardian at Bridgnorth. He became

---

[1] The construction of this sentence is rather difficult. *Latinus* seems to mean "scholar," but one would have expected it to be contrasted with *laicus* as well as with the trade.

a preacher, and edified many. Finally he was sent
to Ireland and there blissfully departed to the Lord.

After these, several Masters (of Arts) entered
the Order, who increased the renown of the
Brethren. One was Brother Walter de Burgh,
concerning whom one Brother saw a wondrous
vision, to wit, how the Lord Jesus, coming down
from heaven, held forth to him a parchment
whereon was written: "The time of thy harvest [1]
is not here but elsewhere." To him the Lord
revealed the (? craft) [2] of a certain woman Religious, who by her feigned visions deceived a wise
Brother, so that he wrote them down. Howbeit
Brother Agnellus, not believing her, bade the
Convent pray that God would reveal to him a
certain matter about which he was troubled. And
lo! in that night it seemed to Brother Walter that
he saw an hind climb rapidly to the top of a
lofty mountain, and two black dogs followed
after her and drove her down into the valley,
and there strangled her: but when Brother Walter
ran to the spot where he thought to find the hind,
he found only a little sack full of blood. When,
therefore, he had told this vision to Brother
Agnellus, he at once perceived that the woman
had been led astray by hypocrisy, and sent to her

---

[1] *Lit.* wheat.   [2] A word is missing here in the MSS.

two discreet Brothers. These, when she had at
last confessed that she had invented what she
said, reconciled her to the truth.

Another Master who entered the Order was
Brother Richard the Norman. When the said
Brother Walter asked him for a word of edification, he replied, after long consideration: "Let
him that would be in peace keep silence" (*Ki
vout estre en pes tenge sey en pes*).

At that time Master Vincent of Coventry also
entered the Order, and, not long after, the grace
of Jesus Christ working with him, zealously prevailed on his brother, Master Henry, to enter it.
He did so on the Feast of the Conversion of St.
Paul, together with Master Adam of Exeter,[1]
of holy memory, and Master William of York,
a fully approved Bachelor of Arts.

Now this Master Adam, renowned throughout
the world, had vowed to do whatever might be
asked from him for love of Blessed Mary, and he
told this vow to a certain anchoress that was his
friend. She revealed his secret to some of her
friends, to wit, a monk of Reading, and another
of the Cistercian Order, and a Friar Preacher,
telling them that by this means they might gain
such a man—not wishing, forsooth, for him to

---

[1] One MS. reads "Oxford."

become a Friar Minor. But, although he was in the presence of one or other of them, the Blessed Virgin did not allow this request for love of her to be made, but it was always put off until another time. Now it seemed to Master Adam that one night he had to cross a bridge where were men holding out nets to the water to capture him, but he, albeit with great difficulty, escaped them, and came to a place of great calm. Accordingly, when by the Divine Will he had escaped those others, he came by chance to visit the Friars Minor, and while Brother William de Colville the elder, a man of exceeding holiness, was talking to him, he said, among other things: "Dearest Master, for love of the Mother of God, enter our Order and uplift our simplicity." And he forthwith, as though he had heard that speech from the mouth of the Mother of God, agreed thereto, and, as is reported, entered the Order to the greatest edification of the clergy.

Master Adam was at that time an associate of Master Adam Marsh,[1] and wore his livery. Not long after, by the grace of God, he sagaciously persuaded him to enter the Order. Now on a

[1] Adam Marsh (*de Marisco*) entered the Order between 1226 and 1232. His learning was famous throughout Europe. He was the friend of Grosseteste and of Simon de Montfort, and the master of Roger Bacon. He died in 1258. A number of his letters are preserved. (See vol. i. of *Monumenta Franciscana*.)

night it seemed to Brother Adam Marsh that they two came together to a certain castle, and over its door was painted the Lord's Cross, and whoever desired to enter must kiss the Cross. Brother Adam of Exeter entered first, having kissed the Cross, and the other Brother Adam, kissing it too, forthwith followed. But the first Brother soon found a spiral staircase and climbed it so quickly that he was swiftly borne from the sight of the Brother that followed. He, following, cried aloud: "Go more slowly, go more slowly!" But the other thereafter was never seen again. And this vision could be clearly understood by all the Brethren then in England, forasmuch as Brother Adam (of Exeter), after entering the Order, went to Pope Gregory the Ninth, and by him was sent, in accordance with his own desire, to preach among the Saracens. But he died at Barletta, after foretelling his death to his companions, and thereafter, as is said, shone forth by noted miracles. But Brother Adam Marsh entered the Order at Worcester, in the fervour of his love of poverty.

After these, there entered the Order Brother John of Reading, Abbot of Osney, who left us an example of all perfection, and Master Richard Rufus, who was greatly renowned in Oxford and Paris alike.

Several Knights also entered it, for example, Sir Richard Gobion,[1] Sir Giles de Merc, Sir Thomas the Spaniard, and Sir Henry of Walpole.[2] Concerning their entrance, the lord King said: "If ye had been discreet in receiving Brethren, if ye had not gained privileges in order to oppress men, and, in especial, if ye had not been greedy in asking, ye could have lorded it over princes."

[1] Cf. p. 32.   [2] In Norfolk.

CHAPTER IV

OF THE ACQUISITION OF PLACES

AFTER this, as the number of the Brethren increased, and their holiness became known, the devotion of the faithful towards them also increased, wherefore they took thought for providing adequate places for them. Accordingly, at Canterbury, Sir Alexander, master of the priests' hostel,[1] bestowed on them a site and built a chapel sufficiently dignified for the time. And because the Brethren refused to take absolute possession of anything, it was made the property of the citizens, but lent to the Brethren at their good pleasure. Very special help was afforded them by Sir Simon Langton,[2] Archdeacon of Canterbury, by Sir Henry of Sandwich,[3] and a noble Countess,[4] an anchoress at Hackington. She cherished them in all ways as a mother cherisheth her sons, discreetly winning for them

[1] Cf. p. 10, note 2.
[2] Brother of Archbishop Stephen.
[3] Warden of that port and of Dover, and a judge.
[4] Loretta, Countess of Leicester, aunt by marriage to Simon de Montfort.

the favour of princes and prelates, whose grace she had gained in a matchless degree.

In London, Sir John Iwyn [1] entertained the Brethren; he bought a site for them and made it the property of the citizens, but with exceeding devotion allotted the usufruct thereof to the Brethren at the good pleasure of its owners. Afterward he himself entered the Order as a layman, and left us an example of completest penitence and highest devotion. This site was added to by Sir Jocelyn Fitzpiers,[2] whose son, a youth of excellent disposition, afterward devoutly entered the Order and more devoutly continued therein until his death. The chapel was built at his own cost by Sir William Joynier,[3] who gave from time to time about two hundred pounds for building other houses, and until his death remained unwearied in spiritual fellowship with the Brethren, conferring on them continual kindnesses. For the building of the infirmary, Sir Peter of Elyland left one hundred pounds at his death. The aqueduct was chiefly provided by the joint gifts of Sir Henry de Frowik, and that right godly youth, Salekin de

[1] A merchant. The site was in the parish of St. Nicholas in the Shambles.

[2] An ex-alderman. His land was in "Stynkynglane," probably so named from its vicinity to the shambles, as above. "Sir" before these names represents *dominus*.

[3] A rich merchant, and sheriff. Cf. p. 52.

E

Basings [1]; howbeit, the King's bounty most generously assisted. Other gifts, moreover, alike of
houses and of money, in extension of sites and in
relief of other needs, gifts many and varied, sources
of wonder to all men, have I seen in London in
my time provided for the Brethren by Jesu most
sweet Himself. Thus it is meet that they should
love and honour Him in especial wise, beyond what
others do, and that for ever.

At Oxford, at the outset Robert the Mercer
received the Brethren and hired for them a house.
Here many "inaugurated" bachelors and many
nobles entered the Order. Afterward the Brethren
hired a house on the site where they now are
from Richard the Miller, who, within a year, gave
the site and house to the citizens of the town for
the use of the Brethren.[2] But the site was small
and too much shut in.

At Cambridge, at the outset the burgesses of
the town received the Brethren, allotting them an
old synagogue hard by the prison. But as the
neighbourhood of the prison was unendurable to
the Brethren — the same entrance serving for
jailers and Brethren alike—the lord King gave
ten marks to buy the rent, payable to his treasurer

---

[1] The surnames de Elyland, de Frowik and de Basings are found
several times in the list of London sheriffs of this century.

[2] See Little, *Grey Friars in Oxford.*

as the rent of that site. And the Brethren built a chapel so exceedingly humble that a carpenter made it in one day,[1] and set up fifteen split tree-trunks. And on the Festival of St. Lawrence, when there were only three Brethren that were clerks, to wit, Brother William of Ashby, Brother Hugh of Bugeton, and a novice named Elias (who was so lame that he was carried into the oratory), they sang the Office solemnly with the music. And the novice wept so much that the tears openly ran down his cheeks as he sang. Now when this novice had made a most holy death at York, he appeared unto Brother William of Ashby at Northampton, and, when he asked him how he fared, replied: "It is well with me; pray for me."

At Shrewsbury, the lord King gave the Brethren a site, and a certain burgess, by name Richard Pride, built them a church, and thereafter one Lawrence Cox other offices. The stone walls of the dormitory, by the decree of the Minister, to wit, Brother William, out of zeal for poverty, he (Lawrence) removed, and made them of mud, with wondrous devotion and docility and at very great expense.

[2] [At Northampton, the Brethren were at first

---

[1] i.e. its wooden framework.
[2] This passage is in the margin of the Phillipps MS., and not in the others at all.

housed by Sir Richard Gobion,[1] Knight, beyond
the East Gate, in land belonging to his family near
the church of Saint Edmund. Here, not long after,
the son of this said patron, John by name, received
the habit. His parents sorely misliked his reception, and the said knight bade the Brethren go
forth and leave his land. To whom the Guardian
with ripe wisdom thus replied: "Let the youth be
placed in the midst, and whichever side he takes,
let that side be established." And they agreed
thereto. The boy accordingly was placed in the
centre of the choir, his parents looking on from
one side, and the Brethren from the other. Then,
when the choice was proposed to him by the
Guardian, Brother John ran towards the side
where the Brethren were, and threw his arms
round the pulpit, crying: "Here I wish to abide."
Then the Brethren made ready to go forth, and
that said lord stood outside the door awaiting
their departure. They came forth ranged as in a
procession, and there followed them last of all
as they went out an infirm old man, holding a
psalter in his hand. Then, beholding their simplicity and humility, the knight, pricked by
Divine inspiration, burst into tears, urgently and
devoutly crying and beseeching that they would

[1] Cf. p. 27.

pardon him, and return, which they did. And this said lord thereafter considered himself as the father of the Brethren. Later on, they were brought into the town by the citizens of the town, and established in the place where they still remain.]

CHAPTER V

OF THE EARLY PURITY OF THE BRETHREN

THE Brethren of those days, having the first-fruits of the Spirit, were serving the Lord, not by rules of men, but by the spontaneous impulses of their devotion. They were content with the Rule alone, and with a very few other ordinances which had been first promulgated in the same year in which the Rule had been confirmed.

Now this was the first constitution which Saint Francis made after the *Regula bullata*,[1] according to what Brother Albert of happy memory said: to wit, the Brethren were not to eat among layfolk, except it were three morsels of meat by reason of the observance of the Holy Gospel.[2] This was because a report had reached him that the Brethren were eating greedily. The Brethren, then, were wont to keep silence until the hour of Terce, and to be so constant in prayer that there was scarce any hour all through the night in which there would

[1] i.e. the Second Rule, confirmed by Honorius III. in November 1223.
[2] St. Luke x. 8.

not be some Brethren in the oratory at prayer.
Moreover, on the chiefest Festivals they sang with
such fervour that at times Vigils lasted the whole
night, and when there were only three or four, or
at most six, of them, they sang solemnly, with
the music. So great, moreover, was their simplicity
and their purity that, if defilement chanced them
by night, they told it among their faults in the
Chapter in the presence of all. And a devout custom
flourished among them of using no oaths at all,
but merely saying: "Know this." As soon as any
was blamed by his Superior, or a companion, he
at once replied, "My fault," [1] often also prostrating
himself on the ground. Wherefore the Master of
the Friars Preachers, Brother Jordan of happy
memory, said that the devil, when he appeared to
him once, told him that "My fault" took from
him all the gain he might have hoped for among
the Friars Minor—that is, because they told their
faults in turn, if one had injured another.

Yet the Brethren were at all times so joyous
and glad among themselves that as they looked
on one another they could scarce restrain their
laughter. Thus, when the young Brethren at
Oxford laughed too often, it was enjoined on one
of them that for each time he laughed in choir

---

[1] *Mea culpa;* the formula in confession.

or at table he should receive the discipline.[1] Now it befell that one day, when he had eleven times received the discipline and yet could not restrain his laughter, he had a vision. The whole Convent was one night, as usual, in the choir, and, as usual, the Brethren were tempted to laugh. Then, lo, the Image of the Crucified which was placed at the entrance to the choir turned toward them as though living, and spake: "They are the sons of Core[2] who in the hour of the Cross laugh and sleep." It even seemed to him as though the Image sought to withdraw its hands from the cross, as though wishing to come down and to depart. Then he beheld the Custodian of the place climb up at once and strengthen the nails, so that it did not come down. Now when this vision was made known, the Brethren were sore afraid, and conducted themselves more wisely, and without excessive laughter.

They were also so zealous for truth that they scarce dared to say aught in an exaggerated way, nor did they conceal their own faults, though they knew that they would be punished if they confessed them.

They made no difficulty about inaugurating places, or abiding in those already established,

[1] A small scourge.　　[2] Cf. Num. xvi. (in A.V., Korah).

or in doing anything else in any sort of way,
provided they knew that it was so enjoined by
their Superior. Thus it befell that Brethren of
noble birth, and notable for other reasons while
in the world, and most beloved in the Order,
allowed themselves without complaint to be set
in places which are now called dreary. One thing
only seemed to sadden that most sweet affection
of their hearts, and this was that they must needs
part one from another. Wherefore the Brethren
often accompanied to great distances those who
were leaving, and, shedding tears copiously as they
returned, gave proof of the affectionate trust there
was between them.

CHAPTER VI

OF THE PROMOTION OF PREACHERS

NOW the Brethren in all things chiefly sought after perfect simplicity and a clean conscience. But, beyond all, in hearing theology taught and in scholastic exercises they were so ardent that, however far they might be from the schools of theology, they did not hesitate to go thither daily barefoot, in bitter cold and deep mud. Wherefore, the grace of the Holy Spirit assisting them, many were within a short time advanced to the office of preaching. First among these was Brother Hugh of Baldock, of happy memory, and Brother Philip of London; Brother William of Ashby also, who had preached the word of God to priests and people alike, not only in sermons but by his devout example.

But that which most promoted the preachers was the coming of Brother Aymon of Faversham, who afforded them the increase of his authority and renown. He was a priest and noted preacher when he entered the Order, together with three other Masters, at Saint Denis on a Good Friday. He, while still in the world, had worn a hairshirt down to his knees, and had shown many other most excellent examples of penitence. Whereby he had at last become so enfeebled and weakly that he could scarce support life unless he used soft and warm things. But a vision after this manner came to him: he was at Faversham, praying in the church before the Crucifix, when lo, a cord came down from heaven, and he took hold thereof and held it fast, and was thus drawn up by it into heaven. When, therefore, he saw the Friars Minor at Paris, mindful of that vision, he summoned up his strength again, and, raising himself against himself, he discreetly prevailed upon his friend Master Simon of Sandwich, and two other men of note, to seek from Our Lord Jesus Christ, while he himself was celebrating Mass, what would be most expedient for their salvation. And when the profession of the Minors approved itself to all simultaneously, they had recourse, for greater assurance, to Brother Jordan, of holy memory, Master of the Friars Preachers, and pledged him on his own soul to give them his advice faithfully. He, as he was inspired by truth, confirmed by his advice the plan they had thought of. Accordingly, they four went to the Minister,

Brother Gregory of Naples, and were received by him at Saint Denis, and clothed with the habit amid great rejoicing, Brother Aymon having first preached on Good Friday from the text: "When the Lord brought back the captivity of Sion, we became like men comforted." [1]

Now on that Easter Day, when Brother Aymon saw a great crowd of folk in the parish church wherein the Brethren heard the Divine Offices— for they had as yet no chapel—he said to the Custodian, who was a layman named Beneventus, that, if he might, he would gladly preach to the people, lest perchance they might communicate while in mortal sin. Then the Custodian bade him preach, on the part of the Holy Spirit. Whereupon he preached so movingly that many delayed to communicate until they had confessed to him. And so he sat for three days in the church hearing confessions, and comforted the folk in no small measure.

This Aymon, as was said above, came to England with the first Brethren, and, alike in preachings and in disputations, and more especially by the goodwill shown him by prelates, greatly advantaged the first Brethren in their simplicity. For he was so gracious and eloquent that he was

[1] Ps. cxxv. 1.

pleasing and acceptable even to those who were hostile to the Order. Wherefore he was made, first, Custodian at Paris and, afterward, Reader at Tours and Bologna and Padua. Moreover, he was sent by Pope Gregory of pious memory on an embassy into Greece to Vatatzes,[1] together with Brother Ralph of Rheims, of happy memory. He [2] caused Brother Gregory of Naples, formerly Minister in France, to be removed from his office, according to his deserts, and, by the just judgment of God, had him imprisoned, while setting free those whom Gregory had unjustly imprisoned. Aymon, moreover, with wondrous zeal for God, cast down Brother Elias,[3] the Minister General, by reason of the scandals which he had caused, and the oppression he had shown towards the most zealous Brethren in the Order.[4] For, by Aymon's agency, many Provinces appealed against him, in the presence of our Father Pope Gregory.

Who, indeed, can presume on his own deserts, who can be safe in his own strength, when he considereth how such personages have come to such a pitch of misfortune? For who in the Uni-

---

[1] Greek Emperor, in 1233.
[2] When Minister General.
[3] Cf. pp. 79–81.
[4] i.e. those known as *Zelanti*, Spirituals, or, later, *Osservanti*, the champions of the literal observance of the Rule.

versity of Paris, or among the clergy throughout France, could compare with Gregory (of Naples) in preaching or high office? Who in the whole Christian world was more gifted or more renowned than Elias? Yet one at the end earned perpetual imprisonment; the other, through disobedience and apostasy, the excommunication of the Pope. Both, however, albeit late, repented.

Now with Brother Aymon there came to England Brother William de Colville the elder, a man of utmost simplicity and exceeding charity. His sister afterward, in the Cathedral Church of Chichester, was most brutally murdered in defending her chastity. For a certain youth, who by reason of her beauty had long desired to find her alone and persuade her to the embrace of love, when he could by no device incline her to his desire, proved how baneful is fleshly delight by killing her in the church. For among those who love after the flesh, as much hatred often springs up at the last as there was love before.

Later on, there came to England many other Brethren of proved worth, who were English by birth, and had entered the Order at Paris. These I saw myself while I was still in the world. One was Brother Nicholas Rufus, an excellent Reader, who afterward, in his zeal for reforming the Order in opposition to Brother Elias, went to the Curia to represent France, together with Brother Aymon. He also described how a certain novice told him that, when he was troubled by constant thirst, and could not sleep at night, there appeared to him one comely to look upon, in the habit of the Brethren, and bade him rise and follow him. When he had done so, he led him into an exceeding pleasant place, and took him into a most fair palace, and gave him to drink a draught most sweet, and said to him: "Son, whensoever thou thirstest, come hither to me and I will give thee to drink." And the novice asked who he was, and he said he was Brother Francis. Then when the novice came to himself he never again endured any temptation from thirst, but, waking up, he felt that he was warmed and comforted both in heart and body.

At that same time came Brother Ralph of (?) Rochester,[1] who by his excellent gift in preaching became most intimate with the lord King of England. But by his end he showed how hostile to God is the friendship of this world, and how opposed to the purity of the Order of Friars Minor it is to be exalted by the favours of the great, and to dwell constantly in the courts of princes.

[1] The MSS. read Rosa, probably for Rofa = Rochester.

There came too Brother Henry of Burford, who, while he was yet a novice, and was the Cantor of the Brethren at Paris, composed these verses in meditation as a help against the temptations which he endured:

Laugh not, thou who Minor [1] art, better tears befit thy part.
Minor thou in name, then see that thy name and acts agree.
Toils endure, let patience bring low thy proud imagining.
Thou dost hate the lowly, say? Patience clears such dregs away.
He who chides thee knows thy needs, hates not thee, but thy misdeeds.
What avail thy vesture poor, squalid food, and couch of boor?
Each is naught if deeds belie what thy habit would imply.
He is but a Minor's ghost who seeks the name without the cost.

Brother Henry afterward for his great worthiness merited to be the special companion of four Ministers General and of four Ministers Provincial in England. He was also, first, interpreter and preacher to the lord Patriarch of Antioch when Legate in Lombardy, and, later, penitentiary to

[1] Qui minor es, noli ridere, tibi quia soli
Convenit ut plores: iungas cum nomine mores.
Nomine tu minor es, minor actibus esto, labores
Perfer, et ingentem minuat patientia mentem.
Nempe cor obiurgat parvam,[2] patientia purgat,
Si quicquam faecis est; si quis te corripit, is est
Qui te custodit; non te, sed quod facis, odit.
Quid tibi cum vili veste, cibove cubili
Porcorum? Certe, tu singula perdis aperte,
Si mentitus eris factis, quod veste fateris.
Umbra minoris erit, qui nomen re sine quaerit.

[1] There is, of course, the familiar play here on *minor*, as meaning lower or lesser.
[2] sc. *mentem.* The readings *pernam* (bacon), *poenam* (punishment), and *peram* (bag for collecting alms in kind) have also been suggested.

the lord Pope Gregory the Ninth, and Custodian in Venice. At one time also he was Vicar for the Custodian in London.

Another who came at that time was Brother Henry of Reresby, who, from being Vicar for the Custodian at Oxford, was assigned as Minister for Scotland; howbeit, his death forestalled this. He appeared after death to the Custodian, saying that, though the Brethren were not damned for their excess in building, they were yet being severely punished; he added also that, if the Brethren recited the Divine Office well, they would be the sheep of the Apostles.

And another who then came to England was Brother Martin of Barton, who often merited to see Blessed Francis. He, later on, was Vicar for the Minister of England, and in many other posts conducted himself excellently. He related how there were five thousand Brethren present at the Chapter General [1] in which Saint Francis bade a house be destroyed that had been built to hold the Chapter. His own brother after the flesh was Seneschal of the Chapter and protected the house on behalf of the Community. And through him Blessed Francis wrote a letter with his own hand—

---

[1] Known as the Chapter of Mats, held at the Portiuncula at Whitsuntide, 1221.

F

standing in the open air in the rain but not getting wet—to the Minister and Brethren in France, that they might rejoice at beholding his writing, and praise God Three in One, saying: "Let us bless the Father and the Son with the Holy Spirit."

On that same day, this our Father rescued unhurt a Brother who had fallen into a deep well; on hearing the report of it, he ran into a church and poured forth prayers. Brother Martin, moreover, told how a Brother who was engaged in prayer at Brescia on Christmas Day during an earthquake was found unhurt under the fallen stones when the church collapsed. This earthquake Saint Francis had foretold, and had caused to be foretold in all the Schools at Bologna through the Brethren, by means of a letter which had bad Latin in it. It lasted for forty days on end before the war with (the Emperor) Frederick,[1] and was so severe that all the mountains of Lombardy were shaken.

Another Brother who came to England was Peter the Spaniard, who was afterward Guardian at Northampton, and who wore a corselet to vanquish enticements of the flesh.[2] He had in

[1] This earthquake of Christmas 1222 is recorded by many chroniclers, one of whom says that it destroyed a great part of Brescia. The prophecy of St. Francis is apparently not mentioned elsewhere.

[2] Cf. p. 15.

his convent a novice who was tempted to quit the Order, whom at last he prevailed upon with difficulty to accompany him to the Minister. As they were going on their way, Brother Peter began to preach to him of the virtue of holy obedience, when, lo, a woodland bird went before them, hopping on the road. Then said the novice, whose name was Stephen: "If it be as thou sayest, Father, command by virtue of obedience that I take this wild bird, and that she tarry for me." When he had done so, at once the bird stayed still, and the novice came up, and took her, and handled her as he would. Forthwith his temptation was entirely allayed, and God bestowed on him a new heart, and he returned straight to Northampton, and was professed (intending) to persevere. Afterward he became an excellent preacher, as I myself saw.

CHAPTER VII

OF THE DIVISION OF THE PROVINCE INTO
CUSTODIES

AFTER this, as the number of their places had already increased, and the Brethren from day to day were multiplying alike in numbers and in merits, and were scattered about, it seemed desirable to divide up the Province into Custodies. At the first Chapter Provincial in London it was accordingly divided into four Custodies, each of which excelled in some one form of saintliness. In the Custody of London, for instance, over which Brother Gilbert presided—he to whom the Blessed Virgin appeared on his deathbed—there chiefly flourished fervour and reverence and devotion at the Divine Offices. In the Custody of Oxford, over which Brother William of Ashby presided, study was the special note.[1]

[In that same Custody of Oxford, over which Brother Peter presided for twelve years, the Brothers did not use pillows until the time when

[1] It is not known which were the other two *original* Custodies.

48

Brother Albert was Minister. Wherefore, when Brother Albert said in the Chapter that the Brethren unsuitably made little mounds to raise their heads, the Custodian replied that they knew well enough that the Brethren were carnally minded, there was no need to tell them so. But neither did the Brethren use sandals, except the sick or weakly, and then only with special leave.

But it chanced that Brother Walter of Madeley, of happy memory, had found a pair of sandals, and had put them on when he went to Mattins. It seemed to him, therefore, that he stood more comfortably at Mattins than usual. But later, when he had gone to bed and was sleeping, he dreamed that he had to go through a certain dangerous pass between Oxford and Gloucester, which is called Baisaliz,[1] where there were wont to be robbers. When he came down into the deep valley, these ran up to him from either side of the way, crying out and saying: "Kill, kill!" Whereat, greatly terrified, he said he was a Friar Minor. But they replied: "You lie, for you walk not unshod." But he, believing himself to be as usual unshod, said: "Nay, but I do walk unshod," and when he calmly stretched forth his foot, he found, in the robbers' presence, that he was wearing these

[1] Name unidentified. Perhaps in the Cotswolds.

said sandals. Then forthwith, roused from sleep by exceeding confusion, he threw the sandals far away into the fields.]

In the Custody of Cambridge, over which Brother Richard of Ingworth presided, the special excellence was the proscribing of money, so much so that, up to the time when Brother Albert visited them, the Brethren of that Custody were not wearing cloaks, as that same Father related. In the Custody of York, over which Brother Martin of Barton presided, zeal for poverty flourished; for he did not allow more Brethren to live in any one place than could be maintained with food by begging alone, without contracting debts.

In the Custody of Salisbury, over which Brother Stephen presided, the feeling of mutual affection was the distinguishing note. He himself was of such a sweetness, such a geniality, and such an exceeding charity and compassion that, in so far as he could, he would allow no one to be made sad. Thus, when he came to die, and the saving Host was brought to him, he beheld in the Host the door through which he must enter,[1] and thus,

---

[1] The same pious play on the words *Hostia* and *ostium* is found in the Eucharistic hymn of St. Thomas Aquinas, "O salutaris Hostia, Quae coeli pandis ostium," which dates from a few years later (about 1262). It may very likely have occurred to other writers also.

singing with a loud voice the *Salve Regina misericordiae*,[1] he passed away blissfully at Salisbury.

In the Custody of Worcester, over which Brother Robert of Leicester presided, there was cultivated beyond all else an unfeigned simplicity. He himself was small in body but large in heart; he ever sought after utmost simplicity, and brought into the Order many simple persons. At last, with strong crying and tears, he rendered up at Worcester his holy and simple spirit to the Lord.

[1] The *Salve Regina* is an antiphon at Lauds in the Little Office of the Blessed Virgin.

CHAPTER VIII

OF THE CHAPTERS HELD BY VISITORS

IT was decreed after this that special Visitors should be sent into England who, in the interest of their Visitations, should hold Chapters. Now the first Visitor for England was Brother William de Colville the elder, who held his Chapter in London while Brother Agnellus was Minister Provincial. Here Sir William Joynier [1] had built a chapel at his own expense, and he then celebrated the entering on its use with memorable pomp.

[And in that same Chapter of Visitation held by Brother Walter de Colville a Brother preached against contracting debts, and said that the case of the procurators [2] was the same as that of a certain priest who was wont each year to keep the Feast of Saint Nicholas. And, lo, it happened that he became so poor that he could not make his usual feast or banquet. And on the very day of the Feast, as he lay abed, while the bells were ringing for Mattins, and meditated what he should

[1] Cf. p. 29.   [2] Cf. p. 17, note.

do, the first bell chimed and said: "How shall I get it?" and the second answered: "On credit, on credit," and while he was considering how he should pay, they both chimed together, and seemed to him to say: "One thing lent here, Another thing there."[1] And, rising, he made a feast on hire. Which speech was approved by the Chapter.]

After Brother Walter came Brother John of Malvern, who was the first to bring the explanation of the Rule according to Pope Gregory the Ninth[2]; he in like manner at London and Leicester and Bristol called together the Brethren, and the novices also, in very great numbers, for the purposes of the Visitation, Brother Agnellus being Minister Provincial. And the scruples of the Brethren as to constructing buildings and having paintings were at that time so strict that he took the strongest measures in the case of the windows in the chapel of the place at Gloucester, and he deprived a certain Brother of his hood because of the pulpit which he had painted, and did the same to the Guardian of the place, because he had allowed the painting.

The third Visitor came by behest of the Minister

---

[1] *Lit.* "What shall I do?" "On credit." "This from one, that from another." (*Ieo ke fray? A crey. Ke del un, ke del el.*)

[2] The Bull *Quo elongati,* 1230.

General, Brother Elias,[1] while Brother Albert was Minister Provincial. He was a German named Wygerius,[2] a man much renowned for legal knowledge and eminent in all worth. He was most intimate with the lord Cardinal Otto, who was then Legate in England.[3] He had received from the Minister General a most severe and subtle rule of procedure. One chief point was that those who in any way concealed anything from him, or used ambiguous words, were to be *de facto* excommunicated, and no one save himself could give absolution from this sentence. Over and above this, he was to carry all accusations to the Minister General.

This caused so great a disturbance among the Brethren everywhere as had never before been known in the Order. For while the Brethren were assembled at London, Southampton, Gloucester and Oxford in very great numbers, and were prolonging their stay there unduly—what with mutual accusations within, and the suspicions of layfolk without—an unbearable storm suddenly sprang up all through the Province. Finally, when the Visitation was somehow completed, a Chapter Provincial was held in Oxford, and an unanimous

---

[1] i.e. not chosen by the Chapter General, as later became the rule.
[2] (?) Wigmund.   [3] Otto came in 1237.

appeal against Brother Elias was preferred. Now, in addition to the Visitation, the Visitor had powers, and had been enjoined in his commission, to do certain other things tending markedly to the detriment of the Brethren.[1] Wherefore he betook himself to the Province of Scotland, and there summoned a Chapter, and desired to hold a Visitation. But the Brethren organised an appeal and, when organised, set it forth, maintaining that, according to the ruling of the Chapter General, they were visited by the Minister of Ireland, and they would not accept any other Visitation.

Thus all the Brethren everywhere were perturbed, and Brother Wygerius no little perturbed himself, so he returned to Germany, taking with him the record of his Visitation. And Brother William of Ashby, whom he had sent to Ireland for the purpose of a Visitation, and who had accomplished his task in one way or another, went forth to join him at Cologne.

Then, when the Brethren had come to Rome, they obtained their petition that the Brethren should be visited in their own places by the authority of the Chapter General, as the Constitu-

---

[1] Especially levying subscriptions towards building the great Church at Assisi.

tion concerning Visitors enjoins. Now Brother Arnulph, penitentiary to the lord Pope, said that, if the devil became incarnate, he would not be able to find a finer-woven and stronger noose for ensnaring souls than was that Visitation.

In the Chapter of the Visitation of Brother Wygerius, Brother Eustace de Merc, of holy memory, was accused on many counts, and was at that time shut out from the Chapter for a day and a half. But a certain other Brother, who had fewer counts against him, was without delay justified. And this Brother said: "O wretch that I am! This man of such noted holiness and such proved devotion and such eminent wisdom is thus visited, and I have thus escaped! Who after this will give aught for the judgments of men?"

CHAPTER IX

OF THE DIVISION OF ENGLAND INTO
MINISTRIES

WHEN some considerable time had passed since the Brethren came to England, the Minister General, Brother Elias, required that the English Province should be split up into two—that is, that there should be one Province of Scotland, and another, as heretofore, of England.[1] For he desired, so it was said, that—just as the Order of Friars Preachers had twelve Priors Provincial throughout the world, after the manner of the twelve Apostles—so he too should have under him seventy-two Ministers, after the manner of the seventy-two disciples. Brother Henry of Reresby was made Minister of Scotland, but he died before the mandate had reached him. Brother John of Kethene, Guardian of London,

[1] The Province of Scotland, which included the north of England, was a separate Province from 1230 (or 1233) till 1239, when it was reunited to England (cf. p. 58). It had a further period of independence, or semi-independence, from 1260 to 1359, when it was again united to England.

succeeded him; he had caused to be established all the places north of York, and afterward received into the Order many honourable and serviceable persons. He brought an especial fervour to the saying of the Divine Office, and in his own behaviour set a pattern of devotion. Brother John received our venerable Father, Brother Albert, in the place at Leicester, with due reverence, and humbly begged him to expound the Rule to the Brethren. After he had ruled the Province of Scotland laudably for many years, on its being joined again to the Province of England, he was made Minister of Ireland by the Minister General, Brother Albert.

[In the time of Brother John, Brother Elias commanded that the Brethren should themselves wash their breeches; the Brethren of the English administration accordingly washed them as had been commanded, but the Brethren of the Scotch administration waited for the withdrawal of the order.]

Moreover, this same Brother John, as I have thought worthy of record, stood firmly by Brother William of Nottingham, Minister of England, of happy memory, in the Chapter General at Genoa, as did also Brother Gregory of Bossells. There, in spite of the opposition of almost the entire Chapter

General, they successfully won their case, to wit, that the privilege granted by the lord Pope of receiving money through procurators [1] should be utterly annulled, and that the exposition of the Rule by Pope Innocent,[2] in so far as it related to points on which it was more lax than that of Pope Gregory, should be suspended. He, moreover, put in a plea for the reconciliation of Brother Elias among all the Definitors [3] of the Chapter General, and obtained his request that he should be admonished by the Brethren not to delay his return to obedience to the Church and to his Order.[4]

Brother John, moreover, was so intent on fostering study that he caused a Bible, annotated throughout, to be bought at Paris, and sent into Ireland. Finally, he was so earnest in consoling Brethren that many of them who were unhappy in other Provinces sought refuge with him and seemed to prosper from being with him. Now when he had been Minister for about twenty years, he was released from office at the Chapter of Metz,

[1] Cf. p. 17, note.

[2] Innocent IV., in the Bull *Ordinem vestrum* (1245).

[3] i.e. the executive officers appointed to conduct the business of Chapters General. (Cf. p. xxxiv.)

[4] Eccleston here seems to have mixed up the Chapters. The suspension of Innocent's exposition took place at one in Metz in (probably) 1254; Elias was excommunicated at one in Genoa in 1244, and died in 1253. The second Chapter at Genoa, here described, must have been in 1249 or 1251. (See Little, *De Adventu*, p. 53, note.)

at which Brother William, Minister of England, was also released.

[When Brother Elias was removed from office, it was provided that there should be only thirty-two Administrations in the Order, to wit, sixteen north of the Alps, and sixteen south. This was with a view to the elections of Ministers General, which appertained to Ministers and Custodians only. If there were so great a number of these voting in elections or decisions—a multitude being a cause of confusion—it would hardly be possible to get through any business quickly that would require the consent of so many persons.]

CHAPTER X

OF THE REMOVAL AND EXTENSION OF PLACES

AS the numbers of the Brethren increased from day to day, those houses and lands which had sufficed for them when they were few could not suffice for a multitude; moreover, by God's providence, there oft entered the Order persons of such degree as seemed rightly to require more honourable provision. Besides this, the Brethren, in their simplicity, had established themselves in some places with so little forethought that it was not a case for extending sites but for removing the houses entirely. Hence it happened that, even during the lifetime of Brother Agnellus, of happy memory, there was much enlarging both of houses and of places. Agnellus, indeed, was so zealous for poverty that he would scarce permit sites to be extended or houses built save in so far as unavoidable necessity demanded. This was clearly shown in the case of the infirmary at Oxford, which he caused to be built so low that the height of the walls was little beyond that of a man, while, until the time of Brother Albert, that house had no guest-house. In like manner he strengthened the dormitory of the London house, when the stone walls had been removed,[1] by mud ones, while the roof remained unchanged. Thus under Brother Albert the place at Northampton was moved, and likewise those at Worcester and Hereford.

Under Brother Aymon also, the sites were extended in several places. For he said that he would rather the Brethren had spacious grounds and cultivated them, so that they might grow their own relishes at home, than that they should beg them from others. This he said on the occasion of the extension of the site at Gloucester, where at first, by decree of Brother Agnellus, the Brethren had cut off a large piece, which they afterward recovered, with great difficulty, from the lord Thomas de Berkeley,[2] through the wisdom and devotion of his wife.

Under Brother William, the places at York, Bristol and Bridgwater were moved, and the places at Grimsby and Oxford were adequately enlarged. Now there was a certain Brother who was such a close friend of Brother William that he was even called "his soul" by some Brethren,

---

[1] Reading, by Professor Little's instructions, *muris lapideis amotis, luto fecit stabiliri*. The MSS. have *amoto*.

[2] Earl of Gloucester. A record of the transaction is in the city archives.

and when he was in trouble Brother William had deigned to write to him with his own hand, out of the exceeding love he bore him. Presuming on this, the Brother said to him that he should accuse him to the Minister General because the London house was not enclosed. And Brother William with glowing ardour replied: "And I shall make answer to the General that I did not enter the Order to build walls." With that same ardour, he caused the roof of the church in London to be set in order, and commanded the bosses of the cloister to be knocked off. Howbeit, he once told his friend, the Brother aforesaid, that it behoved them to make the buildings of a fair size lest the Brethren later on might make them excessively large.

[Brother Robert of Slapton told me that, while the Brethren were in a certain place that was lent them before they had a site, it appeared to the Brother Guardian that Saint Francis came to the place. When the Brethren had met him, they led him into the solar, and he sat there a long time looking about him in silence. The Brethren marvelled, and the Guardian said: "Father, of what art thou thinking?" And the Saint said unto him: "Look round on the house," and he did so, and lo, the whole house was of wattles, smeared with mud and mire. And he said to the Brethren: "Such ought the houses of the Friars Minor to be." And the Guardian took water, and washed his feet, and kissed the Stigmata in his feet. These things, I believe, happened to Brother Robert himself. Now I myself saw a certain renowned preacher who publicly confessed that, through the preoccupation he had had with building the dwellings of a certain place, he had lost the taste for preaching and the devotion that he had been wont to have.

Brother John, moreover, the Visitor of the Order of Friars Preachers in England, said of Brother William of Abingdon that, before he had built the houses at Gloucester, he had an unmatched gift of preaching, and that so great and gifted a preacher ought never to have concerned himself about buildings. Because, as the said Brother John remarked, through that preoccupation he rendered himself so mean that the lord King of England said to him: "Brother William, thou wert wont to speak in such spiritual fashion, but now all that thou sayest is 'Give, give, give.'" And another time, when he had been dealing in flatteries with him while seeking somewhat from him, that same prince called him a serpent.]

[The lord Abbot of Chertsey said to me that

when a Friar Preacher who was a great friend of him asked some logs of him, he gave him one; when he said that it seemed vexatious to him to be troubled about just one log, he gave him another. But when he said that God was a Trinity and therefore he ought to give him three, the Abbot replied: "By God, Who is One, now you shall have one only."]

[When Brother Henry of Burford was professed at Paris, there were only about thirty Brethren in the convent there. At that time they were building in a place called Valvert,[1] where they had put up a long, lofty house that seemed to many Brethren to transgress the rule of poverty of the Order. Wherefore some, and in especial Brother Angeler,[2] besought Blessed Francis that he would destroy it. And lo, at the time when the Brethren should have entered it, by Divine ordering no one went therein, since the entire roof and the walls collapsed even to the floor. And these verses were found written in the place:

> Sheweth heavenly grace by ruin of this place
> That a house less high man should satisfy;[3]

and thus they gave up the site.]

---

[1] Now the Luxembourg Gardens.
[2] Angeler in all the MSS. (?) Agnellus, or Angelo.
[3]
> Gratia divina docuit praesente ruina
> Quod contentus homo sit breviore domo.

The final words, "and . . . site," are added in MS. E. in a very slightly later hand.

CHAPTER XI

OF THE PROMOTION OF READERS

WHEN the place had been enlarged at which study most flourished in England,[1] and where scholars from all over the world were wont to assemble, Brother Agnellus caused a sufficiently dignified School to be built in the place of the Brethren, and gained the consent of Master Robert Grosseteste, of holy memory, to become Reader there to the Brethren.[2] Under him they made advance beyond belief in a short time in disputations and no less in subtle moral science fitting for a preacher to know. When he was removed by Divine providence from his Master's chair to a Bishop's throne, Master Peter became Reader to the Brethren there; he was afterward advanced to a Bishopric in Scotland. To him succeeded Master Roger of (?) Weasenham, who was first Dean of Lincoln Cathedral and afterward Bishop of Coventry. In like manner Master Thomas the Welshman,

[1] i.e. Oxford.
[2] From 1229 to 1235; this famous scholar then became Bishop of Lincoln.

after he had been Reader in praiseworthy fashion
to the Brethren in the same place, was promoted
to be Bishop of St. David's in Wales. These prelates, therefore, always showed themselves favourable to the Brethren in all ways, and promoted their
acts and their good repute greatly in different places.

Thus the good repute and advance in learning
of the English Brethren became so well known in
other Provinces also that the Minister General,
Brother Elias, sent for Brother Philip of Wales
and Brother Adam of York, who became Readers
at Lyons. Brother Albert, moreover, when he
came, made Brother Vincent of Coventry Reader
in London, and his brother, Brother Henry,
Reader at Canterbury. And thus by degrees
Readers were distributed throughout different
places—for example, Brother William of Leicester
at Hereford, Brother Gregory of Bossells at
Leicester, Brother Gilbert of Cranford at Bristol,
Brother John of Weston at Cambridge, Brother
Adam Marsh at Oxford. And the gift of wisdom
so flooded the English Province that before
Brother William of Nottingham was released
from office there were in England thirty Readers
who gave public disputations, and three or four
who lectured without disputation. For he had
assigned students to the different places in the

Universities who should succeed Readers who died or were removed. And now, passing over other things, let us speak briefly of the succession of Readers in the Universities.

The above [1] begin to lecture as Masters, others as Bachelors. At Oxford the first Reader is Adam Marsh.[2] The second, Brother Ralph of (?) Cold-bridge; he had first won praise as Regent in Paris—indeed, he had entered the Order while actually Regent in theology; thence he was appointed by the Minister General to be Regent at Oxford, and there he lectured while still a novice. The third was Brother Eustace of Norman-ville [who had formerly been very rich, and of noble family, Master of Arts and of Canon Law, and Chancellor of Oxford].

[Brother Peter, Minister of England, said that Brother Eustace of Normanville gave greater edification than others as touching his entrance into the Order, because he was of noble birth, and rich, and had been Regent in praiseworthy wise in Arts and Canon Law, and had been Chancellor at Oxford and prompt in beginning his theological course.]

The fourth was Brother Thomas of York, the

---

[1] For notes on all these, see A. G. Little, *Grey Friars in Oxford*, pp. 134–75.
[2] Cf. p. 25, note.

fifth, Brother Richard [Rufus] of Cornwall. He, at the time when Brother Elias was perturbing the whole Order, entered the Order at Paris, and, while the disturbance continued and the appeal was in process, was professed, calmly and devoutly, in England. Thereafter he lectured on the Sentences[1] in a course in Paris, where he was considered a great and marvellous philosopher.

[2] [This Richard, on coming to England, related at a Chapter at Oxford how, when a Brother in Paris was in ecstasy, he had a vision of Brother Giles,[3] a layman, yet a contemplative, sitting in his chair and lecturing on the seven authentic clauses of the Lord's Prayer, his hearers being all Brethren who were Readers in the Order. Then Saint Francis entered, and, after being silent awhile, thus cried out: "O what cause of shame it is for you that such a lay Brother should surpass your merits in heaven above! And because," saith he, "knowledge puffeth up but charity edifieth,[4] many Brethren that be honoured clerks are (? counted) as naught in the eternal Kingdom of God."]

[A certain excellent Reader, who studied with

---

[1] Of Peter Lombard.

[2] This passage is found only in the margin of MS. P.; the last line is damaged, so the reading of it is uncertain.

[3] Blessed Giles of Assisi, one of the first Brethren, and a great mystic.

[4] 1 Cor. viii. 1.

me at Oxford, when a Master was giving a lecture or disputation in the Schools, always made a practice of busying himself with other things instead of with the lecture—such as with compiling original notes. And lo, when he himself had been made Reader, his hearers were so inattentive to him that he said he would as lief close his book each day and depart as he would lecture. And, stricken with remorse, he added: "By the just judgment of God no one will listen to me because I never would listen to any teacher." This Reader, moreover, because he had dealings too constantly with friends in the world, and by reason of their friendship had taken less thought for the Brethren than was his wont, showed others by his example that only in silence and in quiet are the words of wisdom learnt, and that the commandments of God likewise, as saith the Saint, can only be considered by a mind at rest. But, after he returned to his better self and studied in quiet, he made such excellent advance that the lord Bishop of Lincoln said that he could not himself have given the lecture which that Brother did. Wherefore afterwards, as the renown of his uprightness increased, he was summoned to the parts of Lombardy by the Minister General, and was present in the Papal Curia itself, and there considered a great person. Then, at last, as he lay on his deathbed, there appeared unto him the Mother of God, for whom he had always had a devotion, and, the evil spirits being driven away from him, he merited to pass blissfully to the pains of Purgatory, as he himself afterward revealed to a friend. For he told how he was in Purgatory, and had grievous pains in his feet, because he had been wont to go too often to visit a certain pious matron for the sake of consoling her, when he ought to have been absorbed in his lectures and other more necessary occupations. He implored his friend also to have Masses celebrated for his soul. This he did constantly for two years and offered in addition many other prayers.[1]]

[Now the following lectured at Cambridge, not at Oxford: Brother Vincent of Coventry, Brother John of Weston, Brother William the Poitevin, and Brother Humphrey. This last, when he was once ill in Cambridge, as he himself related to me, heard a voice saying to him: "Feel that thou art a stone." Wherefore he lay motionless like a stone. And there came two demons and sat on his left hand, and a good angel stood on his right.

[1] Here is omitted a list of Franciscan Readers at Oxford, written in the Cotton MS. in a later hand; in MS. P. in two different hands; in MS. E. it is omitted. See *De Adventu*, ed. Little, pp. 67–70. Perhaps the most famous name is that of John Pecham, who became Archbishop of Canterbury.

The demons began to anger him with slanders, but the good angel for a long space was silent. At length the demons said: "When the Brethren sit on drinking and chattering in the hour of Compline, then we observe them; when they depart, then we have things to do elsewhere." And the good angel said: "See how great is the malice of the demons! They wish to slay thee with this tedious talk that thou mayest not hereafter praise the name of thy Creator." Then, strengthened by this, he began to sweat, and recovered.[1]]

[1] Here is omitted a list of "Masters of the Friars Minor at Cambridge" (ed. Little, pp. 71–4), given in the Cotton MS. only, in several writings.

CHAPTER XII

OF THE APPOINTMENT OF CONFESSORS

IN addition to these, there were many Brethren who, although they did not hold the office of a preacher or lecturer, yet became confessors to both Religious and layfolk in many places, in consequence of the very welcome favour shown them by the prelates, and in obedience to the commands of the Minister Provincial. Foremost among these in London was Brother Solomon,[1] who was Confessor General to citizens and courtiers alike. When he was Guardian in London after his sickness, as described above, Roger, lord Bishop of London, of holy memory, exacted canonical obedience from him. But when, relying on their long intimacy, he opposed him in friendly fashion, he secured the delayal of it for a time. This lord held the Order in such veneration that he would rise from his seat when any Brother saluted him. Brother Agnellus, therefore, on this occasion,[2]

---

[1] Cf. pp. 17–21.

[2] i.e. of the demand for obedience. The actual passage about the oath occurs in the Bull *Nimis prava* (of 22 August, 1231, i.e. a day later than *Nimis iniqua*) and is repeated in the Bull of the same title of Innocent IV., in 1245.

sent forthwith to the Curia, and obtained the Bull called *Nimis iniqua* on behalf of the Brethren.

Another excellent confessor was Brother Maurice of Dereham, of happy memory. He found a boy who had long been wasting away from a sickness beyond hope of recovery, and, when he had heard his confession, he enjoined him to say the *Hail Mary* thrice daily, and to implore the Blessed Virgin to grant him health, so that he might become a Friar Minor. The boy did so, and was entirely cured. Accordingly, when he was about fifteen years old, Brother Maurice made him take a vow, and live as a Brother among the Brethren until the lawful age (for admission) [1]; when he had attained this, he was clothed without delay, under Brother Agnellus.

At Gloucester, moreover, there flourished Brother Vincent of Worcester, a father to the whole country, who, by reason of his great abstinence and severity towards himself, and his great sweetness and friendliness towards those set under him, was loved by all as though he had been an angel. Wherefore, because of the seriousness of his life and his eminent sagacity, he was afterward advanced to the office

---

[1] Novices might not be received under the age of eighteen save under exceptional circumstances.

of preaching, and became confessor to Roger, lord Bishop of Coventry.

And at Lynn there was Brother Geoffrey of Salisbury, a man of most renowned holiness. In austerity of life he showed himself, if one dare say so, a second Francis; in conformity to virtue and sweetness and in the grace of simplicity, a second Antony. He was so devout and pitiful in hearing confessions that, when he did not see his penitents show any fitting signs of contrition, he would by his own tears and sobs move them powerfully to weeping. Thus it befell with that noble lord, Alexander of Bassingbourn,[1] who made his confession as though he were relating some tale; then, the Brother weeping most bitterly, he was constrained to weep himself. And by his merits and wholesome counsels he was led to purpose entering the Order of Minors, in which intent he died in saintly wise. And after death he appeared to his friend Brother John of Stamford, and when he asked how it was with him, he replied: "My soul fareth as doth a creature which is obedient to its Creator, and whoso doeth that with his whole heart hath rest" (*La meye alme le fet cum creature que est obeysant a sun Creatour; et repose est en celi ke la fit par ducour*).

---

[1] Holder of several high offices under the Crown.

Moreover, he gave him such sublime teaching as to faith in the Sacrament of the Eucharist as no mortal could possibly have compassed.

At Oxford, again, there was Brother Eustace de Merc, of happy memory, who was afterward made Guardian, and finally Custodian, at York. He was wont to relate how Saint Lanfranc, desiring to enter Religion when he was already a leading theologian, put on the dress of a jester and went from Abbey to Abbey to test monkish life. And he came and knocked on the door of the choir with his bauble, and when, in answer, he saw the monks look towards the door and laugh, he said: "God is not here." But when he came to Bec Herluin,[1] and none of the monks paid heed to his knocking, he entered there to take the habit of a lay brother. And when Pope Nicholas was holding the Council against Berengarius,[2] he obtained leave to go thither with his Abbot, and when there, while all were utterly dismayed by the words of the heretic, he besought a hearing. Then he confuted his reasoning so clearly that Berengarius said: "Thou art either Lanfranc or the devil!" And thus he was recognised by the Council.

[1] In Normandy.   [2] In 1059.

CHAPTER XIII

OF THE SUCCESSION OF THE MINISTERS GENERAL

NOW the first Minister General after Blessed Francis was Brother Elias, who had been a notary at Bologna. He was followed by Brother John Parenti [1] of Florence, Minister in Spain, a wise man, and devout, and of extreme austerity. When he was removed from office by the partisans of Brother Elias, the latter was again made General. Now in the Chapter during which the translation of (the body of) Saint Francis took place, the same partisans, whom Brother Elias had allowed to come to the Chapter—for he allowed all who so desired to come thither—wished to have made him General in despite of the Ministers Provincial.[2] Wherefore, taking him from his cell, they carried him on their hands to the door of the Chapter-

---

[1] A learned and saintly Friar, but too mild and retiring to cope with Elias. His sympathies were with the strict Observants, and he has been suggested as a possible author of the *Sacrum Commercium B. Francisci cum Domina Paupertate*.

[2] Eccleston's narrative of this Chapter and the whole Elias episode is unconvincing. See Introduction, pp. xxviii–ix.

H   77

house, and, breaking open the door, wished to set him in the seat of the Minister General. When the General, Brother John, saw this, he stripped himself (of his habit) [1] before the whole Chapter, and then at last the partisans were abashed, and, after the greatest disturbance, gave way. For they would not listen either to Saint Antony, or any Minister Provincial. The people, indeed, believed that the conflict arose because the body of Saint Francis had been translated three days before the Fathers had come together. [2] And five novices who were soldiers, who sat in the Chapter and saw it all, said, weeping, that that turmoil would turn to the great benefit of the Order, because the Order could contain none who were disorderly. And thus it befell, for all those troublers of the peace were sent to perform penance throughout divers provinces.

But Brother Elias betook himself to a certain hermitage, and let his hair and beard grow, and by this semblance of holiness was reconciled to the Order and to the Brethren.

From this Chapter formally-appointed delegates were sent to Pope Gregory for an expounding of the Rule; these were Saint Antony, Brother Gerard

---

[1] *Se nudavit.* **Spec.** *Vitae* gives *habitu se nudans.*
[2] This hurried and furtive action on the part of Elias no doubt told against him.

Russinol, Penitentiary to the lord Pope, Brother
Aymon, who was afterward Minister General,
Brother Leo, who was afterward Archbishop of
Milan, Brother Gerard of Modena, and Brother
Peter of Brescia. And they related to the Pope
what a scandal Brother Elias had caused, because
the Minister General had revoked his order per-
mitting all the Brethren who desired it to come
to the Chapter, and, moreover, how, being wroth
about this, he had caused the translation of the
body of Saint Francis to be carried out before
the Brethren came together. The Pope was sufficiently roused by this, and was very wrathful
against him, until he heard how he was leading
such a strange life in an hermitage. Howbeit,
following on this, in the Chapter at Rieti, when
John Parenti was released from office, the Pope
permitted that Elias should be made Minister
General, and in especial by reason of the close
friendship there had been between him and Blessed
Francis. Afterward, when by his worldliness and
harshness he had upset the whole Order, Brother
Aymon initiated an appeal against him at Paris,
and, against his will, many Ministers Provincial
and much-honoured Brethren from beyond the
Alps came together to hold a Chapter General—
Brother Arnulph, Penitentiary to the lord Pope

Gregory the Ninth, looking after the business of the Order in the Curia.

Accordingly, after lengthy consultation, Brethren were chosen from the whole Order who should frame a scheme for the reform of the Order.[1] When this scheme was settled, it was read aloud in the Chapter General in presence of the Pope, seven Cardinals being also present. After the Pope's sermon—which treated of the golden statue of Nabuchodonosor's dream,[2] from the text: "Thou, O King, didst begin to think what should come to pass"—Brother Elias began to excuse himself, saying that the Brethren, when they chose him as General, said that they wished him to eat gold and have a horse, if his weak health required it, and now they were thus offended and cried shame on him. When Brother Aymon wished to answer him, the Pope would not allow it, until the lord Cardinal Robert of Somercote said to him: "Lord, this man is aged, it is good that you should hear him, for he is sparing of speech." Brother Aymon, then, stood up as one fearful and trembling, but Brother Elias sat on no whit perturbed, as it seemed, and calm. And Brother Aymon began by briefly commending his words as those of a reve-

---

[1] Cf. Jordan, chaps. 64, 65.
[2] Dan. ii. 29. (A.V. Nebuchadnezzar.)

rend father, and continued by saying that, albeit the Brethren had said that they wished him to eat gold, they had not said that they wished him to have a treasury. Moreover, albeit they had said that they wished him to have a horse, they had not said that they wished him to have a palfrey or charger. And forthwith Brother Elias, his patience exhausted, roundly declared that he lied, and his partisans began to make like charges and to add their clamour to his, and those on the other side began to do the like against them. Then the Pope, roused, bade them be silent, saying: "These be not the manners of Religious." Then the Pope sat for a long space as though in silence and meditation, and thus put them all to confusion. Meanwhile the lord (Cardinal) Reginald, Protector of the Order, openly suggested to Brother Elias that he should place his resignation in the hands of the Pope, but he publicly replied that he would not. Then the Pope, first praising the personal character of Elias, and recalling his former friendship with Saint Francis, concluded by saying that he had believed his Ministry to be acceptable to the Brethren, but that, from the time it ceased to be so, as had then been proved to be the case, he decreed that he must be removed. And forthwith he removed him from the office of Minister General.

Then arose such unbounded and unspeakable jubilation as those who merited to take part in it said they had never witnessed.

Accordingly the Pope entered a cell alone, and called the Ministers and Custodians to the election, and, before the votes were written down, he heard them one by one. When Brother Albert of Pisa, Minister of England, had been canonically elected, Brother Arnulph, the Penitentiary, who had been foremost in promoting the whole business, gave out the result of the election, and began a *Te Deum*. And because Brother Elias, as it was said, had never sworn obedience to the *Regula bullata*,[1] for which reason he had a scruple about receiving money, it was at once arranged that he should so swear, and that the whole Chapter should do so, in the same words, and by consequence the whole Order. And thus it was done. Accordingly, after Mass had been celebrated by the Minister General, he said to the Brethren who were not members of the Chapter: "Ye have now heard the first Mass which has ever been celebrated in this Order by its Minister General.[2] Depart now to your places with the blessing of Jesus Christ." In that same Chapter Brother Aymon was made Minister of

[1] i.e. that confirmed by Pope Honorius in 1223.
[2] His predecessors in that office had not been priests.

all England, and Brother John of Kethene, who had been Minister of Scotland, was made Minister of Ireland.

After this, Brother Elias, having chosen the Friary at Cortona as his dwelling-place, went without obtaining leave to the houses of the Poor Ladies,[1] in defiance of the general prohibition of the Minister General; whereby he was seen to have incurred the sentence pronounced against him by the Pope. Then Brother Albert bade him come to him for the sake of obtaining absolution, or bade him at least meet him at some halfway place. When Elias disdained to do this, the report thereof came to the Pope, and, when he found that the Pope desired him, like any other Brother, to obey the Minister General, he could not brook his humiliation, not, forsooth, having learnt to obey, and removed himself to the neighbourhood of Arezzo. Wherefore he was not undeservedly excommunicated by the Pope in public.[2]

Then Brother Albert, showing himself a Minister General worthy of all praise, occupied himself in correcting the excesses of his predecessor, in the Provinces beyond the mountains where the marring of the Order had been more considerable.

[1] The Poor Clares.
[2] Not for disobedience only, but because, as MSS. P. and E. note in the margin, he joined himself to the Emperor Frederick.

He made a good death in Rome, praising the English above all nations in their zeal for the Order.

He was succeeded by Brother Aymon, an Englishman, who studiously devoted himself to carrying on all that Albert had begun. Under him was held the first and last Chapter General of Definitors [1] that there ever was in the Order, by reason of their insolence. For they, forsooth, wished by every method to exclude from the Chapter-house all the Ministers Provincial who were therein, together with the Minister General, and this was done. Wherefore the ruling which had been laid down concerning that Chapter of elected representatives,[2] in the presence of the Pope at the time of the deposition of Brother Elias, and also concerning the canonical election of Custodians and Guardians, was annulled at the next Chapter General by reason of the insolence of those same representatives. For some Brethren wished that Custodians should be entirely abolished in the Order, saying that there was no need

[1] See Introduction, p. xxxiv, and Lempp, *Frère Élie*, p. 134. This Chapter of Definitors, instituted after the Dominican model, was probably held at Montpellier in 1241. But its exclusion of the Ministers, and subsequent independent action taken over the exposition of the Rule by the *quattuor magistri*, raised so much resentment that the experiment was not repeated.

[2] *Lit.* "subjects."

for such an office. Brother Aymon himself was summoned in midwinter by the Protector of the Order [1] and other Cardinals, while he was north of the Alps, and in their presence he replied exceeding well as to the matters charged against him, and won for himself the greatest favour.

In his days there came a command from the Chapter that Brethren should be chosen from the several Provinces of the Order to make notes on doubtful points in the Rule, and refer them to the Minister General. Accordingly there were elected for this purpose in England Brother Adam Marsh; Brother Peter, Custodian at Oxford; Brother Henry of Burford, and certain others. In that very night, Saint Francis appeared to Brother John Bannister and showed him a deep well. When the Brother said to him: "Father, see, our Fathers wish to expound the Rule, do thou much rather expound the Rule to us," the Saint replied: "Son, go to the lay Brethren and they shall expound thy Rule to thee." Accordingly, when notes had been made on some points, the Brethren sent them to the Minister General in an unsealed parchment, beseeching him by the sprinkling of Jesus Christ His Blood that he would

[1] The Cardinal of Ostia.

allow the Rule to stand as it was handed down from Saint Francis, the Holy Spirit dictating it.

Now the above command was most pleasing alike to the Protector of the Order, and to the Brethren beyond sea, and it strengthened the witness that Brother Albert had borne of the English. And Brother Aymon died at Anagni [1]; during his sickness the lord Pope Innocent the Fourth deigned to come and visit him.

[Brother Aymon said that Brethren who were unwilling to come into the convent after they had been ill until they were fairly strong again, for fear they might perhaps not be able to go back to recreation,[2] were like a boy who had to be taught his letters against his will, who, when he had said A, said that, although he knew B as well as he did A, he would in no wise say it, because if he said B the master would bid him say C, and so forth.

He said also that while he was still in the world he had been so delicate that he could not live without manifold devices of clothes and shoes, but that later on he had grown stronger doing without them.

When Brother Aymon returned from the Chapter

[1] Probably in 1243, in the summer of which year the Pope was at Anagni.

[2] I am not clear what this means.

General at which he had been made Minister
Provincial, he had been anxious about his weak
health, and had thought that if he could cross
the mountains he would be anxious no more;
but it happened that he grew strong in the country
of which he had been more afraid, and in France
weaker.]

Brother Aymon was succeeded by Brother
Crescentius, a famous physician, and Minister
at Verona, whose zeal was kindled by charity,
informed by learning, and strengthened by perseverance. For the Brethren in his Province were
so froward towards him that, in the very night
before the Chapter General in which he was
elected, after the complaint that he had made
to the *Zelanti* [1] of the Order concerning the rebellion
of their party, one Brother saw him in a vision,
with his head shorn and having a white beard
hanging right down to his girdle, and heard a
voice from heaven speaking above him in these
words: "This is Mardochai." [2] Now when Brother
Ralph of Rheims had heard the vision, he straightway said: "Assuredly he will be elected to-day as
General." Now when he had faithfully and wisely
served as Minister for some time, he obtained his

[1] Cf. p. 41, note 4.
[2] A.V. Mordecai. The point of the story is obscure.

release from office, and was afterward made Bishop of his native city.[1]

[Brother Ralph of Rheims, an Englishman, came to England after many years of toil, and, after giving himself to the contemplative life at Salisbury for a long space, made a happy end. He related how Saint Francis, when walking along a road in a bitter wind, was becoming faint-hearted, and then summoned up courage and, climbing a mountain, unclad himself and turned to face the wind, and said to himself that it would be well for him if he had on but one tunic.]

To Crescentius there succeeded Brother John of Parma, a Reader, who had given a course of lectures on the Sentences at Paris. He was a leader of the strict party in the Order. He came to England in the time of Brother William of Nottingham, and held a Chapter Provincial at Oxford, and recalled to union those Brethren who had begun to exceed the rest in strange opinions.[2] He proclaimed in all Provinces the obedience and high repute of the English. He reconciled the Brethren at Paris, maintaining in his own person in the University the simplicity of their vocation, and revoking the appeal which

---

[1] Jesi, in the March of Ancona.
[2] It is not known what is alluded to here.

they had made.[1] He ordered that Chapters General should be held alternately north and south of the Alps. At last, being unable longer to bear the burden of his office as Minister General, he obtained leave from the lord Pope Alexander the Fourth to lay it down.

Now this same Father declared that the structure of the Order was built on two walls, to wit, on a good life, and on learning. But the Brethren had made the wall of learning to tower above heaven and heavenly things, so much so that they doubted if God existed, while the wall of good life they had allowed to become so low that it could be said of a Brother as a great eulogy: "He is a safe [2] man." Thus they were seen to be building wrongfully. He desired that the Brethren should protect themselves against prelates and princes by reverence for their profession and by their public merits rather than by Papal privileges, and that they should be Minors among all in humility and gentleness.

[Brother John of Parma, the Minister General, in full Chapter General at Genoa, bade Brother Bonitius, who had been a companion of Saint

---

[1] An appeal to the Pope in the quarrel with the University as to the number of Chairs in Theology to which the Friars were entitled.

[2] *Securus*. Perhaps "quiet."

Francis, tell the Brethren the truth about his Stigmata, because many people throughout the world were doubting about this. And he replied, weeping: "These sinful eyes beheld them, and these sinful hands touched them."]

[Brother Leo,[1] too, a companion of Saint Francis, told Brother Peter, Minister of England, that the vision of the Seraph was shown to Saint Francis in a kind of trance of contemplation, and more clearly than is written in his *Life*, and that many things were then revealed to him which he never communicated to any man alive. Yet, however, the Saint told Brother Rufinus, his companion, that, when he saw the Angel from afar, he was sore terrified, and that he treated him hardly; he told him, moreover, that his Order would last unto the end of the world, and that no man of ill-will could stay long in the Order and that none who hated the Order would live long, and that none who truly loved the Order would come to a bad end. And Saint Francis bade Brother Rufinus wash the stone on which the Angel had stood, and anoint it with oil, and this he did. These things Brother Warin of Sedenfeld wrote down from the mouth of Brother Leo.]

[1] One of the "Three Companions," like Rufinus mentioned below. They were both natives of Assisi.

CHAPTER XIV

OF THE SUCCESSION OF THE MINISTERS PROVINCIAL

NOW the first Minister of England, as has been said above, was Brother Agnellus of Pisa, a man especially endowed with natural sagacity, and marked out by every virtue, rank and honour. After he had with all praise fulfilled the embassy which he undertook on behalf of the prelates of England, together with Brother Peter of Tewkesbury, then Guardian of London, and of the Friars Preachers, in the Roman Curia, he fell sick of dysentery at Oxford. This was caused, it was said, by the cold and toil which he had endured in the cause of making peace again between the lord King and his Earl Marshal [1] in the Welsh Marches, and in travelling throughout England. After the flux had been checked by medicines, a pain in the intestines seized him, and a pain in his side, so that he could scarce keep from crying out. He did, indeed, cry out almost without ceasing for three days on end before he died, "Come, sweetest Jesus!" After he had duly received the Sacra-

[1] Richard, Earl of Pembroke.

ments of the Church, he was asked to give advice
about his successor, and he advised that Brother
Hugh of Wells should be sent to Brother Elias,
and that the Brethren should ask for Brother
Albert of Pisa to be granted them as Minister,
or Brother Aymon or Brother Ralph of Rheims.
And he appointed, so far as it was in his power,
Brother Peter of Tewkesbury as his Vicar. Then
he besought the prayers of each Brother one by
one, and thus, at the close of the commendatory
prayers, which he himself recited together with
the Brethren of the convent, he blissfully breathed
his last.

Now it appeared to his companion, Brother
Walter of Madeley,[1] that there lay in the choir
a dead body, which looked as though it had just
been taken down from a cross. For it too had
five bleeding wounds after the likeness of Jesus
Christ Crucified. He indeed thought that it was
sweet Jesus Christ Himself, but, drawing near and
beholding it from close at hand, he saw that it
was Brother Agnellus.

And after many years, when it was necessary
for the Brethren to remove his body—that is,
when they had pulled down the chapel[2] in the

[1] Cf. pp. 49–50.
[2] In building the new church of the Oxford Friary, in 1246 or
1248.

choir of which he was buried before the altar, they found the leaden coffin in which he lay, and the grave also, full of the purest oil, and the body itself and its wrappings alike uncorrupted and giving forth a most sweet odour.

[It is worthy of record that that venerable man Master Serlo, Dean of Exeter, advised Brother Agnellus seldom to eat outside the convent. It befell once that a certain Guardian, on a day when he had preached to the people, was jesting in talk with a monk after dinner, in the presence of a layman (for they had eaten with the Brethren). Then the layman said privately to one of the Brethren who was his secretary that this did not become one holding office and a preacher. And that same Guardian told me that he would rather have been struck by a lance in his ribs than have set such an example. So greatly were the Brethren zealous for the good repute of the Order, and Brother Agnellus more than all. Thus he would make no exception for the King's secretary, but removed him from Court, and would not allow him to send or receive any gift.]

[Brother Agnellus had for a long time been Minister of England while in deacon's orders, and was unwilling to be advanced to the priesthood, until the Chapter Provincial induced the Chapter

I

General to enjoin it on him. He was so devout in
the Divine Office that, not at Mass only, but also
when saying it in the choir or while out walking,
he was seen continually to weep, yet in such
manner that it could not be observed by his
crying out or groaning or disfigurement of face.
Moreover, he ever said the Office standing, and
sharply reproved a Brother who said his Hours
sitting, after he had been bled.[1] Now when Brother
Agnellus felt death drawing near, he said to
Brother Peter of Tewkesbury: "Thou knowest
all my life," and when Brother Peter said that he
had never made a general confession to him he
smote his head, and, crying out, began to lament,
and forthwith confessed unto him his whole life with
marvellous contrition. Afterward, assembling the
Brethren, he gave them absolution, and when at his
bidding they had begun the commendatory prayers,
he himself closed his eyes with his own hand, and laid
his hands on his breast in the fashion of a cross.]

When Brother Elias heard the news of the
death of Brother Agnellus, he forthwith caused
the Provincial seal, that was stamped with a
lamb bearing a cross, to be destroyed, taking it ill
that the Brethren of England should name any

---

[1] An allusion to the blood-letting performed at regular intervals.
(Cf. p. 99.)

Minister and ask that he might be assigned to them. Wherefore he delayed for nearly a year to send them a Minister. At last, having recalled one whom he had already sent, he ordered Brother Albert of Pisa, who had been Minister in Hungary, Germany,[1] Bologna, the March of Ancona, Treviso, and Tuscany, to go to England and be Minister to the Brethren there. He, then, arrived in England on the Feast of Saint Lucy,[2] and on the Feast of the Purification[3] he held a Chapter Provincial at Oxford, and preached from this text[4]: "Look unto the rock whence you are hewn and to the hole of the pit from which you are dug out." He did all things concerning the Brethren according as he desired and willed, in many ways making trial of the humility and docility, the simplicity and zeal, and the love and patience of the English Brethren. Wherefore, although he had then publicly told the Brethren that they would find him the same to the end as he had shown himself to them in that Chapter, yet thenceforward from day to day he in his wisdom offered the salt of the Gospel with every sacrifice more than is wont, and became entirely changed.[5]

[1] Cf. Jordan, p. 160.   [2] 13 December, probably 1236.
[3] 2 February, probably 1237.   [4] Isa. li. 1.
[5] This difficult sentence seems to show a change in his attitude, his sternness being conquered by the Brethren's obedience. There is perhaps a reference to St. Mark ix. 49.

And so greatly did he afterward praise the English Brethren that he gave himself up to them with his mind's entire affection, and bound them to him by an ineffable compact. For he found them conforming to his will in every scheme of perfection, and ready to go with him to prison and exile for the sake of reform in the Order.

Accordingly, he ordered that silence should always be maintained at table in the guest-house, unless it were with preachers or Brethren of other Provinces. He desired, moreover, that the Brethren should wear old tunics over new ones, both for humility's sake and to make them last longer. He destroyed the stone cloister at Southampton, albeit with great difficulty, as the men of the town opposed it, and he returned to the monks of Reading with exceeding fervour a charter or agreement which had been made between them and the Brethren,[1] to the effect that the monks could not turn the Brethren out at their will, and offered to remove the Brethren himself if they desired. [As to the chapel of that place, because he could not lay it even with the ground, on account of the lord King, who had built it, he hoped that it might be struck by lightning.[2]]

[1] Because it implied ownership.
[2] *Coelitus destrueretur.* This sentence occurs in MS. E. only.

He established Brethren at Chester and Winchester, but with great difficulty.

He received the Bull of the lord Pope Gregory forbidding the Friars Preachers to bind anyone so that he might not enter any order he desired, or to allow their novices to be fully professed before they had completed a year of probation.[1] For they were accustomed to be professed, if they wished it, on the very day of their entrance, as was the case with Brother Robert Bacon, of happy memory.[2] Whereupon the Friars Preachers were greatly perturbed, and obtained from the lord Pope Innocent the Fourth[3] that no Friar Minor should receive those bound to them, and that, if any did so, he should be *de facto* excommunicated; and they themselves promised the same with regard to our probationers. Now they bound men in so many ways, and made known this privilege so extensively, that they scarce let anyone go. But that tribulation did not last long. For Brother William of Nottingham, of happy memory, and Brother Peter of Tewkesbury showed the lord Pope what his predecessor had ordained, and he, saying he had been circumvented,

[1] A similar Bull was addressed at the same time (July 1236) to the Friars Minor.
[2] A Dominican, *d.* 1248.
[3] A Bull, addressed to both Orders, in April 1244.

granted them a revocation thereof, although it was done with vexatious delay.[1]

Brother Albert once said that we ought greatly to love the Friars Preachers, because in many ways they had been helpful to our Order, and had on occasion taught us to be ready in advance to meet coming dangers.

[Brother Albert said that three things in especial exalted our Order—the going barefoot, the shabbiness of clothing, and the spurning of money.

Brother Walter of Reigate said that it was revealed to a Brother in the Province of Saint Francis that the demons hold a council each year against the Order, and that they had then found three ways (of injuring it), to wit, intimacy with women, the receiving of unprofitable persons, and the handling of money.

And Brother Albert, the Minister, was wont to say to one of his companions, Omnebonum[2] by name, when he visited any benefactors of the Order[3]: "Eat, eat, now we can do so safely." But he refrained as much as he could from intercourse with all lay folk.

---

[1] June 1244. This Bull in the main repeated those of Gregory IX. in July 1236, mentioned above, but was addressed to the two Orders together.

[2] The name recalls Ogniben, in Browning's *Soul's Tragedy*.

[3] *Spirituales amici*. This was the recognised name for benefactors of the Order. Sometimes it includes Tertiaries.

In those days it befell that two Brethren of
great renown came to the house of a certain
franklin, who received them with honour and set
before them ample maintenance. And as they
were sitting at dinner, the rector of the church
came in, and blamed them because they had not
betaken themselves to him. When he had strongly
urged them to eat the flesh meats set before them,
and could not break down their temperance, he
said wrathfully: "Eat, eat, for cold kills your
bodies, and gluttony kills our souls," and, rising,
he went out.]

In the Divine Office Brother Albert alway
stood most devoutly, and, with shut eyes, avoided
wandering of mind. In the company of the Brethren
he was ever gay and cheerful, and won to himself
the affection of all.

Thus, when he had once been let blood, together
with the others in the convent, he set forth a parable
of this sort among his companions, chiefly on
account of a certain novice who was present, who
was too wise in his own eyes and presumed to
interfere in matters that did not concern him.
He spake as follows. A certain countryman,
hearing of the great peace in Paradise and of its
many delights, set forth to find where it was,
to see if by chance by some means or other he

could enter it. And when he had at last come to the gate, he found Saint Peter and begged for admission. When Peter asked him if he could keep the laws of Paradise and intended to do so, he said yes, if only he would deign to tell them him. Wherefore Peter told him that the only thing needful was to keep silence. This he willingly agreed to, and was admitted. Then as he went through Paradise he saw a man ploughing with two oxen, one lean and one fat, and the fat one he allowed to go as it would and the lean one he kept on prodding. And the countryman, running up, showed him his mistake. And at once Saint Peter came up, and wanted to turn him out, yet he spared him that time, and bade him be careful. And straightway he went on farther, and saw a man carrying a long beam, and desirous of entering a house, yet he kept on turning the beam lengthwise to the door. The countryman ran up and showed him how he should put forward one end of the beam. And at once Saint Peter came up and wanted by all means to turn him out, yet he spared him that time also. A third time the countryman went forward, and saw a man cutting down trees in a wood, and always he spared the old trunks and crooked oaks, and felled and sawed those that were straight and green and finest.

And, running up, he blamed him. Then at once Saint Peter came up and turned him out.—For the Minister desired that subject Brethren should everywhere have their Superiors in reverence, saying: "Far be it from us that familiarity should breed contempt."

[Brother Adam Marsh narrated how a boy who was too indulgently brought up fell ill, and his father besought him to eat for love of him, as he was his darling son. But the boy replied that he was not his son. In like manner also he answered his mother when she urgently begged him in the same words. And when the father asked whose son he was if he were not his, he replied, angrily and impudently: "I am the son of myself." Thus it is with those who are given up to their own feelings and wills.

In the aforesaid assemblage [1] Brother Albert related a parable against youthful presumption. He said that a young bull was in the habit of going daily at his own will among the fields of grass and corn. One day, about the hour of Prime or Terce, he turned aside towards the plough and saw that the older oxen were plodding on at a footpace and had ploughed little. Then he blamed them and said that he could have

[1] Probably referring to that where the parable of the countryman was told.

done as much in one charge. And the oxen asked him to help them. When he was yoked, he rushed with excessive speed halfway up the furrow, and, worn out, began to pant, and looked back, saying: "How is this? Is it not yet all finished?" And the older ones replied: "Not yet," mocking him as it were. And the young bull said that he could go no farther. Then the oxen told him that they plodded thus at moderate speed because they had to work at all times, and not just on occasion.]

[1] Brother Albert was at Oxford when a young Brother was preaching in the Chapter, and when he had daringly condemned superfluity in buildings and abundance in food, he reproved him as though [2] vainglorious.

He compelled Brother Eustace de Merc to eat fish contrary to his wont, saying that the Order lost many good persons through their indiscretion. And he said that when he was staying with Saint Francis in a certain hospice, the Saint compelled him to eat twice as much daily as he had been wont to eat. Brother Albert was, moreover, so liberal that he severely blamed the Guardian of one convent, and likewise its procurator,[3]

---

[1] This paragraph is in MS. E. only.

[2] (?) *quasi*. Word illegible in MS. St. Francis forbade his Brethren to judge others.

[3] Cf. p. 17, note.

because they had not made more ample provision
for it after exertions on a Festival. He was so
kindly and sympathetic that he made it a matter
of obedience with a weakly Brother to visit his
native place and, if he so desired, to go from place to
place throughout the whole Custody; he said that
he himself would repay the cost of his maintenance, if it were a burden on the Brethren. Now
after he had ruled nobly over the English Province
for two years and a half, he set out, in company
with many others who had been chosen, to oppose
Brother Elias, and, having filled the office of
Minister General, died peacefully at Rome among
the English Brethren.

He was succeeded by Brother Aymon, who,
being most gracious and gentle, studied to keep
the Brethren in all peace and charity. He gave
the habit to the lord Bishop of Hereford, Ralph
of Maidstone, according to a vision which he had
concerning him while he was Archdeacon of
Chester. In his vision, a boy came in while Ralph
was seated and marshalling the clergy in the
synod, and threw water in his face, and he at
once was turned into a pitiable boy. And he came
to the bed in which Brother Aymon lay, and begged
that he would allow him to lie there, and he did
so. And in accordance with this he made a good

end in the Order. Now Brother Aymon was Minister in England for a year and was thereafter elected Minister General.

[Brother Aymon, while he was Minister Provincial of England, said [1] that as it were a sea of troubles overwhelmed the Order when the Brethren caused cemeteries and altars to be dedicated in their own grounds, in order, that is, that they should not be used afterwards for profane purposes. He was so ardent a lover of poverty that at the Chapter Provincial he would sit on the ground, in a very mean and torn habit, with those at the farthest end of the refectory.]

He was succeeded by his Vicar, Brother William of Nottingham, whose election by the community was confirmed by those from whom it had been asked.[2] And Brother William, albeit he had had no experience at all of the lower offices, such as those of Guardian and Custodian, laboured so unsparingly that the fame of his zeal and uprightness was spread abroad throughout all the Provinces.

[Brother William was wont to relate how Saint Stephen, Founder of the Order of Grammont,[3]

[1] The sentence "said . . . purposes" occurs in MS. E. only. The idea is again that of avoiding ownership.

[2] The election was in the hands of the Chapter Provincial, but had to be confirmed by the Minister General. It was quite an exception for anyone to be elected who had not previously held lower office.

[3] Etienne de Muret, d. 1124.

placed a chest in a secret and safe place, and forbade anyone to have access to it while he lived. Wherefore the Brethren were tempted to find out what was in the chest, for the Saint himself desired that all, by his example, should hold it in great reverence. Thus after his death they could not delay, but broke it open, and found nought therein save a paper containing these words: "Brother Stephen, Founder of the Order of Grammont, salutes his Brethren, and prays that they will keep themselves from lay-folk. For just as ye, when ye knew not what was in the chest, held it in honour, so will they with you."]

CHAPTER XV

FINALLY, I think it should be committed to
memory how, while many were yet living who
had planted the vine of the Order of Minors in
the English Province, its shoots had spread forth
so greatly both in that Province and in others
that Brethren were advanced to divers honours
and offices alike in the Order and outside it.
This was especially so with those who had most
humbled themselves.

Brother Nicholas, for example, who, while a
layman, learnt to read in England, afterward
became confessor to the lord Pope Innocent
the Fourth, and, later, Bishop of Assisi. And a
certain boy of very tender years, who was received
as a layman, afterward had a vision of the glorious
Virgin, who placed his finger on his mouth in token
that he should be a preacher and Reader—this
boy did not only become an excellent preacher
and Reader, but was also considered a leader in

the governance of the Order. But who can avail to tell how marvellously those were advanced who, at the first coming of the Brethren, entered the Order with wondrous ardour? When they had been Bachelors of Arts of good standing, and were of noble birth, they wore the hood of a probationer, and later on many of them bore themselves as zealously as commendably in the office of a preacher or Reader, and in the governance of the Order.

Brother Eustace de Merc, who at first was Guardian at Oxford for a long time, and then Custodian at York, kept up until his death his wonted rule of abstinence, vigils and discipline for his own body, while toward others he ever showed the sweetness of an angelic affection. When dying, he repeatedly addressed the Mother of Mercy in these heartfelt words: "By thy Son, O Virgin, by the Father, by the Comforter, be thou present to help me in my dying and my . . . [1] departure."

Brother Robert of Thornham, who was at first Guardian at Lynn and later for many years Custodian at Cambridge, finally obtained permission, with ardour indescribable, to set forth with the Crusaders to the Holy Land; this was after

[1] A word here is illegible in the MSS.

they had gained such matchless (?) (renown)[1] in their weighty task both among layfolk and Brethren. He in death showed us such marked signs of his salvation that none of the faithful ought to doubt of his eternal welfare.

Brother Stephen of Belase was, first, Guardian at Lynn and, later, Custodian at Hereford; he was of such sweetness and such perfection that the zeal of his heart was testified even by tears when he saw the strictness of our profession relaxed. Wherefore, from his exceeding desire for peace, he was released from all office, and had his "fruit unto sanctification and the end everlasting life."[2]

Brother William (?) Cook had been of immense bodily strength, but wore himself out entirely by his early toils in the Custody of London and by other cares; at length he betook himself from the active to the contemplative life and, full of good works, rested in peace.

Brother Austin, brother of Brother William of Nottingham, of happy memory, was at first of the household of the lord Pope Innocent the Fourth. Later, he went to Syria with his nephew, the lord Patriarch of Antioch, and was finally

---

[1] A word here is missing in the MSS.
[2] Rom. vi. 22.

made Bishop of Laodicea. He publicly narrated in the convent at London how he had been at Assisi on the Feast of Saint Francis, and Pope Gregory was there, and how, when he went to preach, the Brethren chanted: "Him the Saint chose as his father," [1] and the rest, and the Pope smiled. Now the Pope in that sermon related how two heretic leaders had been converted at Venice, and had been sent to him with letters from the Cardinals who were his legates in those parts. The letters told how both those heretics on the same night at the same hour saw Our Lord Jesus Christ sitting as Judge together with His Apostles, and all the Orders there are in the world, but they saw nowhere the Friars Minor, nor Saint Francis,—him whom one of the legates in preaching had said was exalted above Saint John the Evangelist by the impression of the Stigmata. Now they beheld the Lord Jesus Himself reclining in the bosom of John, and John in His. And when they assuredly believed that this was shown them in confirmation of their opinion—for they thought the legate had blasphemed, and had been grievously scandalised thereby and had cried shame on the preaching—lo, sweet Jesus with His own hands opened the wound in His side and there

---

[1] Antiphon at Vespers in the Office of St. Francis.

K

was seen most clearly Saint Francis within His breast, and sweet Jesus closed the wound, and shut him up entirely therein. Then the heretics awakened and, when they met each other next day, related their vision each to the other, and, having made public confession to the Cardinals, were sent to the Pope, as already said, and fully reconciled (to the Church) through him.

[O how intensely indebted, O how sweetly over-whelmed by divine loving-kindnesses, O how boundlessly honoured were they who knew so many persons after this sort, having the firstfruits of the Spirit! Who could be guided by their counsels in perplexity, cheered by their consola-tion in sorrow, and stimulated by their example in heavy tasks! O grace unspeakable! O match-less prerogative! O inward sweetness[1] of unex-hausted delight, to enjoy the friendship of such Saints, to be gladdened in the pilgrimage of this life by the special love of such noble persons, to be commended by the favour of so many re-nowned ones!]

After this sermon, some newly-enrolled soldiers came to the Pope, and he laid on each a garland of flowers; thence the custom grew up that all who were to be enrolled as soldiers should receive

[1] *Suavissima viscera.*

their arms on that Feast. And on that Feast the
Pope celebrated Mass in the open air, at a table
outside the church, because he could not be inside
the church for the great crowds of people.

Brother Peter of Tewkesbury, Minister in Germany, the grace of God aiding him, so stoutly
defended the condition of the Order against the
King and the legate and many false Brethren,
that the fame of his action went forth into many
Provinces, and his proved zeal for invincible
truth.[1]

He had the privilege of enjoying the special
friendship of the lord Bishop of Lincoln,[2] from
whom he often heard many secrets of wisdom.
For instance, he once said to him that unless the
Brethren fostered study and gave themselves up
studiously to Theology, it would assuredly befall
us as had befallen other Religious, whom, alas!
we see walking in the shades of ignorance.

Moreover, he said to Brother John de Dya that
he would provide himself with six or seven fit
clergy from his district to whom he might give
benefices in his church—who, for instance, although they knew no English, might preach by
their example. Whence it is certain that he did
not refuse those whom the Pope appointed, and

[1] It is not known what is alluded to here.   [2] Grosseteste.

the Cardinals' nephews, on the ground of their
not knowing the English tongue, but because
they sought only after temporal gain. Wherefore,
when a lawyer said to him in the Curia: "The
Canons decree this," he replied: "Nay, the canines
decree it." [1] He arose, and confessed it in English,
on his bended knees, before the youths presented
to him by the Cardinals, and he beat his breast
with weeping and wailing; and thus they withdrew
in confusion.

Again, when the Chamberlain of the lord Pope
sought from him the thousand pounds with which
he had been charged for his business in the Curia,
and desired him to borrow them from the
merchants, he replied that he would not give
the merchants an occasion for falling into mortal
sin,[2] but that, if he returned safe to England, he
would deposit them in the House of the Templars,[3]
otherwise he would never receive a penny.

Again, he said to a Friar Preacher: "Three
things are necessary to temporal welfare—food,
sleep, and a jest." He also bade a certain melan-
choly Brother to drink a cup full of the best wine
as a penance, and, when he had drunk it, albeit
most unwillingly, he said to him: "Dearest Brother,

[1] *Canones* and *canes* (dogs). Rendering suggested by Professor
Little.
[2] i.e. by usury.   [3] Often used as a bank.

if you more often had a penance of this sort you would indeed have a better conscience."

Brother Peter also related how, when some clerks of the household of the Archbishop Edmund [1] besought him on behalf of a kinsman of theirs who was a forester, the Saint replied: "If his cart be broken, out of regard for your prayers I will have it mended, and if it cannot be mended, I will buy a new one, but know for certain that I will never alter his station in life." Moreover, that same holy prelate replied, when some valuable jewels were offered him, and he was advised by his people to accept them: "If I should take them I should hang! [2]—*entre prendre e(t) pendre* there is but one letter's difference."

Again, this same Father, Brother Peter, related how when Robert, lord Bishop of Lincoln, at his first promotion to his see, was very short of horses, his seneschal came to him as he sat at his books, and informed him that two white monks had come to present him with two very fine palfreys. When the seneschal worried him by urging him to accept them, and to pronounce the monks exempt, [3] he agreed no whit, nor moved from his place, but

[1] Edmund Rich, *d.* 1240.
[2] *Si prenderem, penderem;* he repeats it in French.
[3] i.e. from episcopal jurisdiction, so that accepting the palfreys could not be considered a bribe.

said: "If I were to accept them, they would drag me to hell at their tails."

[The lord Bishop of Lincoln, Robert Grosseteste, was once so seriously annoyed because a Minister would not allow a Brother—one whom he had entertained formerly—to abide in his guest-house, that he refused to speak to any Brother, even to his own confessor. Then Brother Peter told him that if he were to give all his goods to the Brethren, and did not give them his heart's love, the Brethren would not care for the gifts. And the Bishop began to weep, and said: "Of a truth ye do wrong, for ye afflict me exceedingly, for I cannot help but love you, although I have shown such a countenance toward you." And the Brethren ate at his table at his side, and yet he would not speak to them.

The Bishop said to Brother Peter that places standing over water are not healthy, unless on a lofty site. He said, moreover, that it pleased him greatly when he saw the sleeves of the Brethren patched. And he said that pure pepper was better than ginger in a sauce. He said also that he rejoiced when he saw that his scholars did not care about his lectures, so long as he had prepared them carefully, because an occasion of vainglorying was thus taken from him, and he lost nothing of his merit.]

Now Brother Mansuetus, legate of the lord Pope
Alexander the Fourth, told that same Father in
the same place that, on the day when the Bull [1]
was read in audience in which the lord Pope
Innocent the Fourth had decreed eight sentences
against the Friars Preachers and Friars Minor, he
lost his speech, save that he afterward said: "Thou
hast rebuked man for his iniquity." [2] And he
invoked Saint Francis again and again, for while
in health he had said that from no other Saint
had he gained so many petitions. Now the lord
Alexander the Fourth, when he was Cardinal of
Ostia, had said beforehand that he had been
assured that the Lord would speedily remove the
Pope from their midst because of the favour
which he had shown to the detriment of the Order.
Indeed, at his death, all his household deserted
him, except the Friars Minor, and the same was
the case with Pope Gregory, and Honorius, and
with Innocent, [3] at whose death Saint Francis was
present in person. The said Brother Mansuetus
also said that no beggar, not to say no mortal
man, dies more wretchedly and meanly than does
a Pope.

[Brother Mansuetus said that, on the very day

---

[1] *Etsi animarum* (November 1254).
[2] Ps. xxxviii. 12.   [3] Innocent III.

of his election, the lord Pope Alexander the Fourth
suspended the Bull which the lord Innocent had
given out against the Preachers and Minors, and
afterwards, as his first act as Pope, revoked it.
For Innocent had decreed that all the Brethren
should be excommunicated if they received a
parishioner of any one of them on any feast day
to hear the Divine Offices, and the like.]

He also told how a Brother who was standing
in prayer in a garden in Sicily beheld an exceeding great army of five thousand horsemen advancing
into the sea, and the sea hissed as though they had
all been made of molten bronze, and one of them
told him that it was the Emperor Frederick entering into Mount Etna. Now Frederick died just at
that time.[1]

Again, Brother Mansuetus related how, when he
was a boy of about ten years old, he was taught
by the Friars Minor to hold the Eucharist in very
special reverence. Thus, in order that he might
worthily communicate on Easter Day, he fasted,
while yet a child, nearly the whole of Lent. And
lo, on that very Easter Day, when all the people
were communicating, a man who was steeped in
utmost crime and infamy, by name Execius,[2]

---

[1] 13 December, 1250. Etna was believed to be a mouth of hell.
[2] (?) possibly Ezzelino, the notorious tyrant.

drew near to make his communion. Then, when he had received communion without any of the reverence due to it, he straightway turned aside, and sat on a bench, and began to chatter with the bystanders, taking no more heed than if he had a mere morsel of bread in his mouth. And lo, Brother Mansuetus saw the Host come forth of his mouth and fall to the ground in a great open space. Then he went at once to the priest, a right venerable man, and told him what he had seen; he bade him seek the Host on the spot where It had fallen. When the boy sought, he soon found It in the same place, although people had gone on passing over that place as they went to communion and returned. Then the boy received with reverence the said Host and all those that remained on the altar after consecration, and was unspeakably strengthened in his faith.

Moreover, Brother Peter, Minister in England, related how, when he was a very intimate member of the household of the lord Geoffrey le Despenser, it chanced that he came on a time to the said house, and the lord's son, a little boy named John, came up to him in the friendliest way, as he was always wont to do. But after the child had gone with his lady mother into the chapel, and been present while Father Peter was celebrating Mass, when he returned to the house, he ran away from the said Father, nor could he by any means be induced by his mother to approach him. And when she asked the reason why he ran away from the priest, he said that he had seen him devour an infant on the altar in the chapel, and feared lest he might do the like to him.

[Brother Warin of (?) Orwell entered the Order when but a youth, and later made such progress that, greatly admired by all, he was the formally-appointed Reader in many places, and bore himself discreetly in intimacy with the great, and conducted the business of the Order commendably, and waxed great beyond compare in the office of a preacher and in study and contemplation. At length in the same ninth hour [1] he died before the altar at Southampton, while holding and embracing the crucifix. And a certain Brother named John, who had died long before, appeared at Salisbury to Brother Simon of Wimborne, and said that all was well with himself, and that Brother Warin had, without any delay, passed through Purgatory and gone to Our Lord Jesus Christ.]

Indeed, the English Province had attained to such a degree of perfection that Brother John of Parma, the Minister General, would often say,

[1] i.e. as the Death on the Cross.

THE GREY FRIARS TOWER, KING'S LYNN

while he was in England: "Would that a Province such as this had been set in the midst of the world that it might be an example to all!" That same Minister General held a Chapter of the Province of England at Oxford, in which he confirmed the Provincial Constitutions about frugality, and poverty of buildings. And when he had given the Brethren the choice of confirming the Minister Provincial in office or of releasing him, the whole community besought him that he might be confirmed.

Now this Brother William once said that, when the lord Bishop of Lincoln of holy memory, who was at that time Reader to the Friars Minor at Oxford, had preached in a Chapter of the Brethren on poverty, he had placed begging as the next step on the ladder of poverty to the embracing of heavenly things. He had, however, said privately to Brother William that there was yet one step higher, to wit, to live by one's own labour. Wherefore he said that the Beguines are of the most perfect and holy Religious life, because they live by their own labours and do not burden the world with demands.

This Father worthy of remembrance also said that there was a certain novice who desired to practise abstinence and said to the novice master that he proposed to try gradually what he could do. And his master gladly gave him permission. And after he had begun for some time, and was often asked by his master how he did, and replied that he was well, he began at last to fear that he might grow weak. He said so to his master, who replied: "For God's sake, quickly eat and drink, or thou wilt fail, because thy faith faileth. Thus Peter too, fearing, sank."

Moreover, he said that the mind and intention of Saint Francis in the Rule ought to be considered, otherwise, just as hairs in the beard grow without being noticed, so superfluities grow in the Order. And we must strive against the current of the world more than is (strictly) necessary, otherwise it will drag us down lower than we think, just as a river does when folk wish to cross it and make a straight track for the opposite bank. Besides this, he said that a man does not know if it will be troublesome to him to be moved from a place, save by experience, just as he does not perceive that hairs are attached to his head save when they are pulled.

He was himself a most close student of the Holy Scriptures and in studious wise assisted those studying them. At meals outside the refectory he wished there should always be reading, and with chiefest love he reverenced the Name Jesus, and most devoutly meditated upon the words of the Holy Gospel. In consequence whereof, he compiled some very helpful canons on the *Unum ex quattuor* of Clement,[1] and arranged for the exposition made by the same Clement to be written out in full in the Order. In his meditation after Mattins especially he sat for a very long space, nor would he turn his attention to hearing confessions or giving counsel at night, as his predecessors had done. He said also that, as it is worse to give a false rule in making anything than to make it badly, so base opinions about things done in the Order are worse than imperfect works. He was most cautious in believing any tale unless the narrator was ready to repeat it in the presence of many hearers, and he strove to avoid above all things the vice of suspicion.

He most carefully refused friendships with the great, and with women, and also with wondrous loftiness of soul made light of the wrath of powerful personages in the cause of justice. He once said that great persons ensnare their friends with their counsels, and that women, inasmuch as they are false and spiteful, turn the wits of even the devout by their flatteries. With all diligence he sought

[1] *A Concordance on the Four Gospels,* by Clement of Llanthony.

to restore the good repute of those that were of
ill fame so long as he considered they had repented,
and with the utmost sagacity he strove to comfort
the hearts of the desolate, especially of those
holding office in the Order.

Now after Brother William had ruled the Pro-
vince of England for about fourteen years, he was
released from office at the Chapter of Metz and,
on behalf of the Chapter General, was sent to the
Pope. But when, in company with the Minister
General, he had reached Genoa, his companion,
Brother Richard, was stricken by a pestilence
which arose, and, while others fled, Brother
William stayed there to be a help to his companion.
Then he was stricken together with him, and died.
Then the Brethren in England, hearing that he
had been relieved from office, and not knowing
of his death, called together a Chapter Provincial,
and re-elected him. When the Minister General
heard that this had been done, rather on an impulse
of affection than from a reasoned judgment, he
summoned the Chapter again through his Vicar,
Brother Gregory of Bossells, and ordered that
they should never again re-elect anyone who had
been released by the Chapter General. He demanded, moreover, the confirmation of the election of a Brother from Brother John of Kethene

and Brother Adam Marsh and Brother John of Stamford. And Brother Peter of Tewkesbury was elected, and his election confirmed there and then.

[When Brother Elias was dismissed, Pope Gregory was asked if he might then be re-elected, and the Pope said, "No."]

[When some Brethren desired that debts should in no wise be contracted, Brother William said to me that the Brethren ought not to bind themselves in any way to repay, nor to fix in advance a given time for repayment, but they might lawfully bind themselves to use their best efforts to cause payment to be made.

He said, moreover, that there were an hundred cases in which Brethren might lawfully contract debts, and also that a Brother did not sin if he dispensed with his own hand the money of another person in alms.

[1] Brother William said that, when he was staying for some time in the convent at Rome, and the Brethren had no relish but chestnuts, he became so fat that he was sore ashamed. He told me, again, that when he was being brought up in his father's house, and poor boys came begging for alms, he would give them some of his own bread, and take from them a crust, because it seemed

---

[1] In the MSS. this paragraph follows on after the next.

to him that hard bread, begged for the love of God, was sweeter than the dainty fare on which he and his companions were nourished. Wherefore, that they might make their own food thus sweet, the little boys went and begged it from one another for the love of God.

Another thing he said was that, after a Visitation, he always needed to take a little recreation, to turn his mind from what he had heard. He told me that sweet Jesus would raise up a new Order to stir up ours, and this I think was fulfilled in the Order of Penitence of Jesus Christ. For he had before this recommended to our Brethren the Brethren of the Order of Saint Austin, at the Chapter at Stamford. And, long before, he had everywhere received as housemates of our Brethren the Carmelite Brethren, whom the lord Richard de Grey brought into England when Earl Richard returned from Syria.[1] Robert, lord Bishop of Lincoln, rejected the Brethren of the Order of Crossbearers, and in like manner the Brethren of the Holy Cross were rightly refused.[2] The Brethren of the Order of the Trinity came to England long before. They were founded by John, a Master in Theology, in the time of Innocent

[1] Richard, Earl of Cornwall, brother of King Henry, and afterwards King of the Romans. He returned in 1242.

[2] This sentence occurs in MS. E. only.

L

the Third, by Divine guidance, Christ Jesus appearing to him while he was celebrating Mass before the Bishop and clergy of Paris.

Brother Peter was the first to receive the Brethren of Penitence of Jesus Christ, and recommended them at the London Chapter; they had their beginning in Provence at the time of the Council of Lyons, their founder being a certain novice who had been rejected.[1] In the third year of the administration of Brother Peter the Brethren of the Order of Martyrs came to England; their founder was one Martin, who at Paris had been like an official fool of the German nobles.]

[2] A certain wise Brother said that there be two things which Brethren love much, and a third to which they are much given; the two which they love are poverty without penury and patience without being humiliated; the third to which they are much given is prayer without devotion.[3]

---

[1] Raymond Attanulfi. He was rejected by the Friars Minor while a novice on account of weak health.

[2] This sentence occurs in MS. E. only.

[3] An irrelevant paragraph is omitted here, as it occurs in MS. P. only, added by another hand.

THE CHRONICLE OF
BROTHER JORDAN

MAINZ IN THE MIDDLE AGES
(*After a print by Hollar*)

THE
CHRONICLE OF BROTHER JORDAN

PROLOGUE

To the Friars Minor established throughout Germany Brother Jordan of Giano in the Vale of Spoleto wisheth perseverance in good in this present life, and in the life to come everlasting glory with Christ.

FORASMUCH as many Brethren have been edified when at divers times they heard me give some account of the manner of life of the first Brethren sent into Germany, I have been often asked by many persons to write down what I have related, and other things that I can recall to mind, and to make notes of the years in which Brethren were sent to Germany and in which this or that happened. And because, according to Holy Scripture,[1] "it is like the sin of witch-craft to rebel and like the crime of idolatry to refuse to obey," I have decided to yield to the devout desire of the Brethren. I am chiefly impelled thereto by Brother Baldwin of Brandenburg, who, both of his own accord and at the

[1] 1 Kings xv. 23.

bidding of Brother Bartholomew, then Minister of Saxony, offered himself as scribe.

Accordingly, in the year of Our Lord 1262, after the Chapter held at Halberstadt on the third Sunday after Easter,[1] we remained in the place where the Chapter had been held, I relating and Brother Baldwin writing, as I (determined) somehow to satisfy the desire (of the Brethren).[2] And this indeed is well, and I myself should wish it. But if allowances must be made—for, as ye know, I am not learned enough for the task—it was ye who forced me to it. As to the dates, if I have anywhere been mistaken about them through forgetfulness, being only mortal, and now old and infirm, I ask pardon of the reader, and admonish him, whenever he finds me to have erred, of his charity to correct and amend it. In like manner, we wish well to him who will adorn with more polished words the style of the writer and the barbarity of his language. It is enough for us to have furnished material to excellent masters of language, skilled in the art of composition.

When I compare my own lowly state, and that of the others who were sent into Germany with

---

[1] *Dominica Jubilate;* so called from the Introit for the day, which begins *Jubilate Deo.*

[2] The text of MS. B. is imperfect here; Boehmer supplies the words *fratrum statui.*

me, with the condition and renown of our Order as it now is, I am inwardly confounded, and extol the Divine mercy in my heart, and I am constrained to extol before you that saying of the Apostle [1] : "See your vocation, Brethren, that not many are wise according to the flesh," who might have built up our Order by their wisdom, "not many mighty," who showed that it was to be passionately preserved, "not many noble," on account of whose favour they have undertaken to observe it. "But the foolish things of the world hath God chosen, that He may confound the wise, and the weak things of the world hath God chosen that He may confound the strong, and the mean things of the world, and the things that are contemptible, hath God chosen, and the things that are not, that He might destroy the things that are, that no flesh should glory in His sight."

Wherefore, that our glorying may be in God, Who by His wisdom devised this Order and through His servant Francis set it as an example to the world, and not to any glorying in man, it will be clearly set forth in the following pages when, and how, and through whom the Order came down to us.

---

[1] 1 Cor. i. 26–9.

1. In the year 1207, Francis, a merchant by trade, was pricked in heart, and, by the inspiration of the Holy Spirit, entered on a life of penitence in a hermit's dress. As the manner of his conversion is sufficiently set forth in his *Life*,[1] we pass it over here.

2. In 1209, the third year of his conversion, he heard in the Gospel the words that Christ spake to His disciples whom He sent forth to preach, and straightway cast aside his staff and wallet and shoes, and changed his habit, putting on that which the Brethren now wear. He became an imitator of Gospel poverty, and a zealous preacher of the Gospel.

3. In the year 1219,[2] the tenth year of his conversion, Brother Francis, in a Chapter held at Saint Mary of the Little Portion, sent Brethren to France, Germany, Hungary, Spain, and the other Provinces of Italy into which the Brethren had not yet penetrated.

4. Now the Brethren who came to France,

---

[1] Probably alluding to the *Legenda Prima* of Celano, which his language here recalls.

[2] This is the correct date, though Kom. reads 1216. There were two Chapters at the Portiuncula, 1217 and 1219, when missionary expeditions were arranged: those in the former year, apparently, to the infidels, in the latter, to Christian countries (cf. chap. 7). "Tenth" is probably the copyist's error for "thirteenth" (cf. chap. 10), and *fr.* (*frater*) for the usual *b.* (*beatus*). (See Boehmer, Introduction, pp. lxxii–iii.)

when asked if they were Albigenses, replied that they were, not understanding what Albigenses meant, and not knowing that they were heretics. So they were thought to be heretics themselves. But when the Bishop of Paris and the Masters there at length read their Rule, and saw that it was founded on the Gospel and was Catholic, they consulted the lord Pope Honorius on the matter. And he pronounced their Rule authentic, and confirmed by the Apostolic See, and made known by his Briefs that the Brethren were peculiarly the sons of the Roman Church, and true Catholics, and thus he freed them from the suspicion of heresy.

5. To Germany there were sent Brothers [1] . . . John of Penna with about sixty or more Brethren. When they entered the borders of Germany, and, not knowing the language, were asked if they wanted shelter, or food, or other things of the sort, they replied, " Ja," [2] and in this way they received a good welcome from divers folk. When they saw that by saying " Ja" they were kindly treated, they decided that they ought to reply " Ja" to whatever they were asked. So it befell that when they were asked if they were heretics,

[1] The name of a Brother seems to have dropped out here.
[2] "Yes."

and if they had come to Germany in order to infect it in the way they had perverted Lombardy,[1] they replied " Ja." Whereupon some of them were beaten, some imprisoned, and others stripped and led naked to the local court,[2] and made a sport for men to mock at. Then the Brethren perceived that they could win no fruit in Germany, and returned to Italy. From this experience, Germany was considered by the Brethren to be such a ferocious country that only those inspired by a longing for martyrdom would dare to return thither.

6. The Brethren who were sent to Hungary were brought thither by sea by a certain Bishop of Hungary. As they were walking in groups through the fields, the shepherds set their dogs at them, and, without saying anything, kept on striking them with their pikes, turning aside the point. When the Brethren debated among themselves why they were thus being tormented, one said: "Perchance it is because they want to have our outer tunics." They gave these up, but the shepherds went on beating them. So he added: "Perchance they want our under tunics also." And they gave them up, but still the blows went on.

[1] In Germany, Lombardy was regarded as a hotbed of heresy.
[2] Reading *choram* in place of *choream*, as Fr. Auweiler suggests. See Ducange.

And he said: "Perchance they want our breeches as well." And when they gave these up the shepherds ceased beating them, and let them depart naked. One of those same Brethren told me that he had lost his breeches fifteen [1] times in this way. And since, overcome by shame and modesty, he grieved more for the loss of the breeches than of his other garments, he fouled those breeches with cowdung and other filth, and by that means the very shepherds sickened at them, and let him keep the breeches. After they had suffered these and many other despites, they returned to Italy.

7. Of the Brethren who went to Spain five were crowned by martyrdom.[2] But I am not sure whether or not these five Brethren were sent out by that same Chapter or the preceding one, like [3] Brother Elias and his companions sent beyond sea.

8. Now when the life and history of these martyr Brethren aforesaid had been brought to Blessed Francis, he heard himself praised therein, and saw the Brethren glorying in their martyrdom. Whereupon, as he held himself in utmost scorn, and

[1] Perhaps a copyist's error for the more likely six or seven, which MS. B. reads in chap. 18, where the incident is recalled.

[2] In Morocco, 16 January, 1220.

[3] Boehmer has here questionably substituted *ut* for *et* of MS. B. *Et* would extend the doubt that Jordan admits about the other mission to that of Elias also.

contemned praise and glorying, he put aside the history and forbade it to be read, saying: "Let each glory in his own suffering and not in that of another."

Thus all that first sending forth came to nought, perchance because the time for sending was not yet come, since "there is a time and opportunity for every business." [1]

9. Now Brother Elias was made Minister Provincial by Blessed Francis while beyond the sea. A certain clerk named Cæsar was converted by his preaching, and received into the Order. This Cæsar, a German, native of Speyer, and a subdeacon, was a pupil in theology under Master Conrad of Speyer, a preacher of the Cross, and afterward Bishop of Hildesheim. Cæsar, while he was still in the world, was a great preacher and follower of evangelical perfection. As a result of his preaching in his own city, some married women laid aside their ornaments, and began to live humbly, and their husbands were wroth thereat, and wished to hand him over to be burnt as a heretic. But he was saved by Master Conrad, and returned to Paris. And afterwards, crossing the sea with a duly organised expedition,[2] he was

---

[1] Eccles. viii. 6.
[2] This appears to be the meaning of *sollempni facto passagio.*

converted to the Order by the preaching of Brother
Elias, as related above, and became a man of
great learning and influence.

10. Matters being thus arranged, the Blessed
Father bethought him that he was sending forth
his sons to sufferings and toils, and desired not to
appear to be seeking a quiet life for himself while
others were toiling for Christ. For he was ambitious in spirit, and was fain that none should
surpass him in the way of Christ, but rather that
he should surpass them all. So then, after sending
forth his sons to possible dangers and among the
faithful, he himself, glowing with love for the
Passion of Christ, faced the certain dangers of the
sea, crossing over to the infidels, and betook himself to the Soldan.[1] This he did in the same year
in which he sent forth the other Brethren, to
wit, the thirteenth year of his conversion. But
before he reached him, he suffered many despites
and insults, and, not knowing their language, kept
on calling out as they were beating him, "Soldan,
Soldan!" And thus he was brought to the Soldan,
and was by him honourably received, and humanely
treated in his weakness. And when he could gather
no fruit among them, and was disposed to return,

[1] The contrast here is between *incerta* and *certa* (of dangers) and
fideles and *infideles*. St. Francis's mission was in 1219–20. His interview
with Malek-el-Khamil, Sultan of Egypt, is often depicted in art.

he was, by the Soldan's orders, conducted by an armed escort to the Christian host, which was then besieging Damietta.

11. Now when Blessed Francis was going over-sea, in company with Blessed Peter of Catania, a doctor of law and jurisprudence, he left behind two Vicars. These were Brother Matthew of Narni and Brother Gregory of Naples.[1] He established Matthew at the Portiuncula, that he might abide there and receive into the Order those that were to be admitted, and sent Gregory to travel about Italy strengthening the Brethren. Now, in obedience to the first Rule, the Brethren were in the habit of fasting on Wednesdays and Fridays,[2] and, by permission of Blessed Francis, on Mondays and Saturdays, and were eating fleshmeats on every day when meat was lawful. But these Vicars, together with some of the elder Brethren in Italy, held a Chapter in which they decreed that the Brethren on flesh days were not to eat flesh meats that had been procured for them, but only such as might be offered them of their own accord

---

[1] Cf. Eccleston, pp. 41–2.

[2] *Feria quarta*, etc. *Feria*, which originally means a feast or rest day, was first used of the days in Easter week, all of which counted as feast days. The name was then extended to ordinary weekdays; each Sunday (*dominica*) being a feast, Monday was *feria secunda*, Tuesday (as in the first sentence of Eccleston) *feria tertia*, and so on. Saturday was *sabbatum*.

by the faithful. And, beside this, they decreed that they should fast on Mondays and on two other days, and that on Mondays and Saturdays they should not provide for themselves milk foods, but should abstain from them unless they happened to be offered them by the faithful in their devotion.

12. Now a certain lay Brother was wroth at these enactments, that they had dared to add anything to the Rule of our holy Father, and he crossed oversea without the Vicars' permission, taking these enactments with him. And he came to Blessed Francis and first of all confessed his wrongdoing before him, and sought pardon because he had come to him without leave granted, urged thereto by necessity, because the Vicars whom he had left behind had dared to impose new decrees over and above his Rule. He added, moreover, that the Order throughout Italy was perturbed alike by the Vicars and by other Brethren who were essaying innovations. These enactments were read over while Blessed Francis was at table, and had fleshmeats set before him to be eaten, and he said to Brother Peter: "My lord Peter, what shall we do?" And he replied: "Ah, lord Francis, whatever thou wilt, for thine is the power." Because Brother Peter was a man of education and of noble birth, Blessed Francis in his courtesy

called him "lord" to pay him honour, [and he, on the other hand, humbling himself before his spiritual father, paid him the same deferential observance.[1]] And they observed this mutual deference oversea as well as in Italy. So at last Blessed Francis concluded: "Then let us eat the things set before us according to the Gospel (precept)."

13. At that time there was beyond sea a certain sorceress who predicted many things truly, whence in their language she was called "truth-teller." [She said to the Brethren who were with Saint Francis[1]]: "Return, return, for through the absence of Brother Francis the Order is being perturbed and rent and broken up." And this was done. For Brother Philip, who was a champion of the Poor Ladies,[2] obtained leave from the Apostolic See in defence of the Ladies and for the excommunication of those that troubled them. This was contrary to the desire of Blessed Francis, who preferred to win everything by humility rather than by legal powers. In like manner also Brother John of Conpello [3] got together a great number of lepers, both men and women, and withdrew himself from

---

[1] The words in brackets here and below are incorporated by Boehmer from G.

[2] The Poor Clares. He had been appointed one of their Visitors.

[3] Probably "de Capella," as MSS. Kom. and G. read.

the Order, wishing to become founder of a new Order. He composed a Rule and appeared before the Papal throne with his followers to have it confirmed. And, beside these, certain other beginnings of disorders arose in the absence of Blessed Francis, as that soothsayer had foretold.

14. Then Blessed Francis, taking with him Brother Elias and Brother Peter of Catania and Brother Cæsar (whom Brother Elias, Minister of Syria, had, as related above, received into the Order), and other Brethren, returned to Italy. And there he came to understand more fully the causes of these disturbances, and addressed himself, not to those who caused them, but to the lord Pope Honorius. Accordingly, our Father in his humility lay outside the door of the lord Pope's chamber, not daring to knock on the door of so great a prince, but patiently waiting till he should come forth of his own accord. And when he came forth, Blessed Francis did him reverence and said: "Father Pope, God give thee peace!" And he: "God bless thee, son!" And Blessed Francis continued: "Lord, seeing that thou art a great lord, and often hindered by great affairs, poor men often cannot have access to thee nor have words with thee whenever they have need. Thou hast given me many popes

M

Give me one, with whom I may speak when I have need, who in thy place shall hear my concerns and those of my Order, and discuss them." And the Pope said: "Whom wilt thou that I give thee, son?" And he: "The lord Cardinal of Ostia." And he granted it. When, therefore, Blessed Francis had told the lord Cardinal of Ostia, his own pope, the reasons of his distress, the Cardinal at once revoked the letters given to Brother Philip, and Brother John with his followers was dismissed in disgrace from the Curia.

15. Thus, by the grace of Our Lord, the disturbers of peace were speedily quieted, and he reformed the Order in accordance with his own decrees. And Blessed Francis, perceiving Brother Cæsar to be learned in the sacred Scriptures, entrusted to him the task of adorning the Rule, which he himself had drawn up in plain language, with the words of the Gospel. And this he did. Now the Brethren had heard divers reports about Blessed Francis, some saying that he was dead, some that he had been killed, others that he was drowned, and thus very many of them had been perturbed. But when they knew that he was living, and had even now returned, it seemed to them in their joy that a new light had dawned upon them. Then Blessed Francis straightway

summoned a Chapter General at Saint Mary of the Little Portion.[1]

16. Accordingly, in 1221, on the tenth day before the Kalends [2] of June, in the fourteenth (year of the) indiction, on the Festival of Pentecost, Blessed Francis held a Chapter General at Saint Mary of the Little Portion. To this Chapter there came, in accordance with the custom then prevailing in the Order, both those who were fully professed and the novices, and the number of the Brethren who had then assembled was reckoned at three thousand.[3] At this Chapter there was present the lord Cardinal-deacon Rainerius, together with many other Bishops and Religious. At his command, one of the Bishops celebrated Mass. And Blessed Francis is believed to have read the Gospel at Mass, and another Brother the Epistle. As the Brethren had no buildings to contain so many Brethren, they abode in a vast plain surrounded by booths, eating at twenty-three tables and sleeping in groups, all well-ordered, separate, and amply spaced. The people of the

---

[1] The famous "Chapter of Mats."

[2] These dates are incorrect. Pentecost in 1221 fell on 30 May, and in the ninth indiction. The indictions were recurring periods of fifteen years; the word indiction, with a number, was also used for a specified year and its place in the cycle. This system of reckoning time was in use at the Papal Court.

[3] Eccleston and the *Spec. Perf.* say 5000.

district supplied this Chapter with bread and wine most readily and in abundance, rejoicing at the assembling of so many Brethren, and at the return of Blessed Francis.

In this Chapter, Blessed Francis took as his text[1]: "Blessed be the Lord my God, Who teacheth my hands to war," and preached to the Brethren, both teaching them virtues, and exhorting them to patience and to setting an example to the world. In like manner a speech was made to the people, and both people and clerks were edified.

Who can avail to set forth what love, patience, humility, obedience and brotherly gaiety there were then among the Brethren? Never have I seen a Chapter like it in the Order, either for the numbers of the Brethren or the distinction of those who served them. Although the number of the Brethren was so great, the people so joyously brought them all manner of provisions that, after seven days of the Chapter, the Brethren were compelled to shut the door and refuse all gifts, and to remain there two extra days in order to use up all that had been already offered and accepted.

17. Now at the conclusion of this Chapter— that is to say, when the Chapter was about to be dissolved—Blessed Francis bethought him that

[1] Ps. xviii. 35.

the edification brought by the Order had not reached Germany. And because Blessed Francis was then in feeble health, Brother Elias spake aloud to the Chapter whatever he desired to be said from himself, and Blessed Francis sat at the feet of Brother Elias and pulled him by his tunic. Then Brother Elias bent down to him, and heard what he wished, and, raising himself, said: "Brethren, thus saith the Brother" (signifying Blessed Francis, who was called "the Brother" *par excellence* by the Brethren): "there is a certain land named Germany, in which there are devout Christian men. These, as ye know, often[1] go through our land with long staves and great candles, sweating in the sun's heat, singing praises to God and His Saints, and visit the shrines of the Saints. And because the Brethren sent to them at times returned after being evil entreated, the Brother does not compel anyone to go among them. But if there are any inspired by zeal for God and for souls who desire to go, he will give them the same mandate, or, indeed, a wider one, than he would give to those going oversea. And if there be any who desire to go, let them rise, and withdraw to one side." And, kindled by longing for martyrdom, about ninety Brethren rose, offering

[1] See corrigendum, at end of Boehmer, of *sepe* for *spe* in text.

themselves to death, and, withdrawing apart, as they had been bidden, waited to know which and how many of them were to go, and in what manner, and when.

18. There was at that time in the Chapter a Brother who used in his prayers to beseech the Lord that his faith might not be corrupted by the heretics of Lombardy,[1] and that he might not apostatise therefrom through the brutality of the Germans, and that the Lord would deign mercifully to deliver him from either of them. When he saw these many Brethren rise and be ready to go into Germany, he thought that they would straightway be martyred by the Germans. Now he regretted that he had not even known by name the Brethren who were sent to Spain and martyred,[2] and desired to avoid the same happening to him with these as had with those. Wherefore he rose from among the assembly and went to them, going from one to another and asking: "Who art thou and whence art thou?" thinking that, if they should happen to be martyred, it would be a great glory for him to be able to say: "I knew this one and that one." One of them was a Brother named Palmerius, a deacon, who was afterward made Guardian at Magdeburg;

[1] Cf. p. 134.   [2] Cf. p. 135.

he was a joyous and mirthful man, native of Monte Gargano in the parts of Apulia. When that inquisitive Brother came and asked him who he was and what was his name, he replied: "My name is Palmerius," and then, laying his hand on him, he added: "Thou too art one of us and wilt go with us,"—desiring to take him with him among the Germans, as to which that Brother had already besought the Lord many times that He would send him wherever He willed except to them. So, shuddering at the name of Germans, he replied: "I am not of your company, but I came to you desiring to have known you, not with the intent of going with you." And Palmerius in his jesting way proved stronger than he, and held him back, and, though he protested and struggled, dragged him down to the ground with him, and forced him to sit with himself among the others.

Meantime, while this was going on, and that inquisitive Brother was detained in that company, he was assigned to another Province, and it was announced: "Such-and-such a Brother is to go to such-and-such a Province." Then, while those ninety Brethren were awaiting their answer, Brother Cæsar, a German, and native of Speyer, as already said, was assigned to Germany as

Minister, and given power to choose from those ninety those whom he would. And when he found that inquisitive Brother among the others he was exhorted by the others to take him too with him. And when that Brother was unwilling to go among the Germans and firmly said: "I am not one of you, I did not rise with the intent of going with them," he was brought to Brother Elias. Now the Brethren of that Province to whom he had been assigned, hearing this, sought to retain him, all the more because he was not strong and the land to which he would go was cold. But Brother Cæsar was minded by all means to take him with him. And Brother Elias ended this contest by saying: "I bid thee, Brother, on holy obedience, consider finally whether thou desirest to go or to be released." But the Brother, thus bound by obedience, hesitated what to do, fearing to choose because he scrupled lest, if he chose, he might seem to be following his own will. He feared to go by reason of the ferocity of the Germans, lest he might lose patience in sufferings and so might imperil his soul. Thus, perplexed between the two courses, and not finding any counsel in himself, he went to a Brother who had been proved by many trials—that Brother who had fifteen times [1]

[1] Cf. p. 135.

lost his breeches in Hungary, as related above—
and sought counsel from him, saying: "Dearest
Brother, thus am I bidden to do, and I fear to choose,
and what to do I know not." And he: "Go to
Brother Elias and say, 'Brother, I desire neither
to go nor to remain, but I will do whatever thou
shalt bid me.' And thus thou shalt free thyself
from this perplexity." And this he did. When
Brother Elias heard it, he bade him, by virtue
of holy obedience, go to Germany with Brother
Cæsar. Now this Brother is Jordan of Giano, who
writes this for you, who in this manner came to
Germany, who escaped the fury of the Germans,
which he had dreaded, who was among the first,
with Brother Cæsar and the other Brethren, to
plant the Order of Minors in Germany.

19. The first Minister of Germany was Brother
Cæsar. In his anxiety for fulfilling profitably the
mandate laid upon him, he took with him Brother
John of Piano Carpine,[1] a preacher in Latin and
in the Lombard speech, and a German called
Barnabas, an excellent preacher in the German and
Lombard tongues, and Thomas of Celano, who
afterward compiled both a First and Second *Life*
of Saint Francis. He took also Joseph of Treviso,

---

[1] Now called Magione; near Perugia. He became very important
in the Order. See Boehmer, pp. 21–3, notes, for details of several of
these Friars.

and a Hungarian named Abraham, and Simon, a Tuscan, son of the Countess of Colazon, and Conrad, a German clerk, and Peter, a priest from Camerino, and James and Walter, both priests, and Palmerius, a deacon, and Brother Jordan of Giano, a deacon. Likewise certain lay Brethren, to wit, Benedict of Soest,[1] a German, and Henry, a Suabian, and many others whose names I do not remember. They were in all twelve clerks and fifteen laymen. Brother Cæsar, then, chose out these, and, because in his devotion he was unwilling to leave Blessed Francis and the other holy Brethren, he obtained permission from Blessed Francis to divide the companions assigned him among our houses in Lombardy, there to await his summons, while he himself abode for nearly three months in the Valley of Spoleto. And when he made ready to take his journey into Germany, he summoned his Brethren and sent before him Brother John of Piano Carpine, and Brother Barnabas, and several others, to Trent, to prepare a place for himself and the Brethren, the remaining Brethren following by threes and fours.

20. Thus the Brethren, arriving in successive groups, were assembled in Trent before the Feast of Saint Michael, and, during the six days on which

[1] In Westphalia.

they thus came one after another, were graciously received by the lord Bishop of Trent. And on the Feast of Saint Michael Brother Cæsar preached a sermon to the clergy and Brother Barnabas to the people. And a citizen of Trent, named Peregrine, a rich man, learned in the German and the Lombard speech, as a result of their preaching gave the Brethren new outer tunics and undergarments, and sold all the rest of his goods and gave them to the poor, and was received into the Order.

21. After this, Brother Cæsar called together his Brethren in Trent and gave them an exhortation as to observing humility and patience. Then, leaving [1] there some Brethren for the edification of the people, he grouped the others in twos and threes, setting one over temporal affairs and another over spiritual, and sent them before him to Botzen. And there the lord Bishop of Trent for several days maintained the Brethren as they arrived in succession, and gave them leave to preach in his diocese. From Botzen they came to Brixen, and were graciously received by the Bishop of that place. From Brixen they entered on the mountainous regions, and reached Sterzing

[1] The words *relictis* to *alios* have dropped out of MS. B. and have been supplied from G.

after the dinner-hour of the (?) folk[1] there. And as the folk had no bread at hand, and the Brethren knew not how to beg (in their tongue), they hoped that they would come by evening to some place where they might be refreshed by the piety of the inhabitants. And they came to Mittenwald,[2] where in great scarcity they moderated, or rather intensified, the evil of wretched hunger and their thirst with two small mouthfuls of bread and seven turnips, with gladness of heart. And they consulted together how they might fill their empty bellies so that they might pass a quiet night after the toil of walking seven miles, and they decided to drink of the water of a clear stream flowing by, that their empty bellies might not complain. When it was early morning, they arose, famished and empty, and pursued the way on which they had started. After they had walked to the halfway milestone, their eyes began to fail, and their limbs to give way, and their knees to be weakened, from fasting, and their whole bodies to be enfeebled. Wherefore, by reason of their extreme hunger, they stripped fruits from the thorns and from divers sorts of trees and herbs which they found by the way. And because it

[1] Reading *hominum* for an uncertain word in the MS.
[2] Jordan is here confusing with some other name—(?) St. Jodok or Gries. (There is a Mittenwald between Brixen and Sterzing.)

was a Friday they feared to break their fast. Howbeit, they seemed to be a little refreshed by the fact that they carried the fruits of various trees and brambles, so that, if extreme necessity drove them to it, they would have somewhat to eat. In this manner, now halting, now going on slowly, they reached Matrei[1] with difficulty. And behold, God, to Whom is the poor man left,[2] was mindful of His own poor ones, and provided that, on entering the town, they should meet two charitable men, who bought them two deniers' worth of bread. But what was that among so many? And as it was then the season for turnips, they begged turnips, and supplemented by turnips their shortage of bread.

22. When they had made their meal, by which they were rather filled than refreshed, they went on, and thus, passing by towns and castles and monasteries, came to Augsburg. Here they were most graciously received by Siboto, Prince-Bishop of Augsburg, and the Vidame,[3] his nephew, a Canon of the mother church.[4] The Prince-Bishop of Augsburg himself bore himself so affectionately toward the Brethren that he greeted each one

[1] On the Brenner.
[2] Ps. x. 14.
[3] *Vice dominus.* Perhaps Bishop's Vicar.
[4] *Major ecclesia.* This term often, but not invariably, denotes the cathedral of a city.

with a kiss and dismissed him with a kiss. And the Vidame received them with such affection that he left his palace and established the Brethren therein.[1] Beside this, they were graciously received by clergy and people alike, and greeted with respect.

23. In the year 1221, about the feast of Saint Gallus,[2] Brother Cæsar, first Minister of Germany, assembling his Brethren in Augsburg to the number of thirty-one, and holding his first Chapter on their entrance into Germany, sent out the Brethren thence into the different provinces of Germany. He sent Brother John of Piano Carpine and Brother Barnabas, the preachers, to Würzburg. Thence they passed to Mainz, Worms, Speyer, Strasburg, and Cologne, showing themselves to the people, and preaching the word of repentance and preparing abodes for the Brethren that were to follow.

24. In that same Chapter, Brother Cæsar sent Brother Jordan of Giano, with two companions, Abraham and Constantine, to Salzburg. And they were graciously welcomed by the Bishop of that place. And he sent three other Brethren to Ratisbon with Brother Joseph. Brother Cæsar followed in the footsteps of these who went on in advance,

---

[1] This was their first house in Germany.

[2] 16 October. The Confessor after whom the Swiss Canton is named (*fl. circ.* 550–627).

confirming the Brethren in good by his word and example.

25. In the same year, when Brother Cæsar came to Würzburg, he received into the Order a youth named Hartmodus, who was clever and educated. As the Italians did not know (how to pronounce) his name, they called him Andrew, because he was received into the Order on Saint Andrew's Day. He in a short time took priest's orders and became a preacher and was later on made Custodian of Saxony. In like manner he also received a layman named Rüdiger, who was afterward made Guardian at Halberstadt, and master of spiritual discipline to Blessed Elizabeth,[1] teaching her to observe chastity, humility and patience, to watch in prayer, and toil in works of mercy. In like manner he also received a layman named Rudolph.

26. In 1222 Brother Cæsar had already admitted so many Brethren, both clerks and laymen, that he assembled the Brethren from neighbouring cities and held his first Chapter Provincial in Worms. And because the place wherein the Brethren had been received was small, and not suited for celebrating or preaching when such numbers were present, they took counsel with the Bishop and

[1] St. Elizabeth of Hungary.

Canons, and assembled for celebrating and preaching in the mother church; the Canons crowded themselves into one choir and left the other choir to the Brethren. A Brother of the Order celebrated Mass, and one choir vied with the other in singing, so that they conducted the Divine Office with great solemnity.

27. From this Chapter Brother Cæsar sent two Brethren with letters for those in Salzburg, who had not come to the Chapter, bidding them come to him if they so desired. But they, who had utterly given themselves up to obedience, so that they desired to do nothing at their own pleasure, were no little perturbed by the condition made in the letter, that is, "if they so desired." And they said: "Let us go and enquire why we have been thus written to, since we desire nought save what he desires." Then they set forth on their way, and, as they came to a certain town for the sake of a meal, they went throughout the town in couples begging, and were answered in German: "*God berad*," which, being interpreted,[1] is "God help you," or rather "May God provide for you!" One of them, perceiving that no gift accompanied this saying, thought and even said: "This *Got*

---

[1] Lit. *latine dicitur*. So again below. A form of declining to give help. The *d* and *t* are preserved as in the text.

berad will be the death of us to-day." And he went on before his comrade, who was begging in German,[1] and began to beg in the Latin tongue. And the Germans answered: "We do not understand Latin. Speak to us in German." And the Brother, pronouncing badly, said: "*Nicht diudisch*," which, being interpreted, is "No German," "do I know" being understood. And he added in German: "*Brot durch Got*." [2] But they said: "'Tis a marvel to hear thee, speaking German, say thou knowest no German!" And they added: "*Got berat*." And the Brother, rejoicing in spirit, and smiling, and feigning not to understand what they said, sat him down on a bench. Then a man and woman, glancing at one another, and smiling at his audacity, gave him bread, eggs, and milk. Then when he saw that he could assist his Brethren and himself in their need by such a profitable pretence, he went to twelve houses doing the same, and begged as much food as sufficed for seven Brethren.

Continuing on the same road, they came before Mass on the Feast of Pentecost to a certain town. There they heard Mass, and one of them made his Communion. And the townsfolk were so moved by the simplicity and humility of the Brethren

---

[1] So G., adopted by Boehmer. MS. B. reads *cottidie* (daily).
[2] i.e. "Bread, for God's sake."

N

that they bent the knee before them and venerated their very footprints. Thence, passing through Würzburg and Mainz and Worms, they came to Speyer. There they found Brother Cæsar and many Brethren assembled, and were by them, as was customary, most warmly welcomed, and they were most devoutly rejoiced by their coming. And Brother (Cæsar), when taxed by the Brethren with having so written, excused himself and explained his meaning and thus satisfied them.

28. In the same year, which was the second since the arrival of the Brethren in Germany, Brother Cæsar, Minister of Germany, assembled the Brethren in Cologne and in the aforesaid cities, and there was such a shortage of priests among them that one priest novice celebrated for the Brethren in Speyer and in Worms on the great Festivals, and heard their confessions. Wherefore, in that same year, he caused three to be advanced (to priest's orders), to wit, Palmerius, of whom we have spoken above, and Abraham the Hungarian and Andrew the German, who had been called Hartmodus before.

29. In 1223, on the third day before the Kalends of December,[1] the Rule of the Friars Minor was confirmed by the lord Pope Honorius the Third.

[1] 29 November.

and Brother William, both Englishmen; Brother
Giles, a clerk from Lombardy; Brother Palmerius
and Brother Reynald of Spoleto, both priests;
Brother Rüdiger, a German layman; Brother
Rokkerus, a layman; Brother Benedict, a German
layman; Brother Thietmarus, a layman, and
Brother Emanuel of Verona, a tailor.[1]

35. These all came to Hildesheim and were
received by a Canon, Henry of Tossem, and well
refreshed. Then, on their presenting themselves
to the lord Bishop Conrad, a great preacher and
theologian, he gave them a splendid reception.
This Bishop, I say, assembled the clergy of his
city, and made Brother John of Piano Carpine,
the first Custodian of Saxony, preach to a great
host of them. When the sermon was ended, the
lord Bishop commended Brother John and the
Brethren of his Order to his clergy and people,
and gave them authority to preach and hear
confessions in his diocese. And many were moved
to penitence by the preaching and example of the
Brethren, and entered the Order. One of these
was Bernard, son of the Count of Poppenburg, a
Canon of the mother Church, and another was
Albert, a schoolmaster and man of letters, and
there was one named Ludolph, and a certain

[1] For another tailor in the Order, cf. Eccleston, p. 22.

soldier. But when a disturbance arose there in consequence of several Brethren leaving the Order, the goodwill of the people towards the Brethren cooled to such an extent that they gave them alms with vexation and, as it were, turned away their faces when they saw them begging. But, on a sudden, by the help of God's providence, the favour they had lost revived, and the people returned to their first love for the Brethren.

36. In 1223, Brother John of Piano Carpine, with a view to spreading the Order, sent many discreet Brethren to Hildesheim and Brunswick and Goslar and Magdeburg and Halberstadt.

37. In 1224, a Chapter Provincial was held in Würzburg on the Assumption of the Blessed Virgin,[1] the Custodians, Guardians, and preachers being assembled. And they released from office Brother John [of Piano Carpine, Custodian of Saxony[2]], and sent him to Cologne, and appointed Brother James, Custodian of Alsace—a man gracious, gentle, modest, and pious—as second Custodian of Saxony. With him they sent several of the elder Brethren of the Order, both clerks and laymen, who speedily made great advance in the favour of clergy and people by their humility and example.

---

[1] 15 August.   [2] The words in brackets are supplied from G.

38. In that same year Brother Albert of Pisa, Minister of Germany, seeing the gains in Saxony and that from Saxony they could pass through Thuringia to the Rhine, sent Brother Jordan, Guardian of Mainz, with seven Brethren, to find houses in Thuringia and establish the Brethren in suitable places.

39. Accordingly Brother Jordan, with his Brethren from Mainz, started on his way toward Thuringia on the sixth day before the Kalends of November [1] and arrived at Erfurt on Saint Martin's Day. And because it was winter, and not a time for edification, by the advice of the townsfolk and some of the clergy, the Brethren were established in the house of the priest who served the lepers outside the walls, until the townsfolk should make better arrangement for their welfare.

40. Now the Brethren who were sent with Brother Jordan were the following: Brother Hermann of Weissensee, a novice who was a priest and preacher; Brother Conrad and Brother Henry of Würzburg, novices who were sub-deacons; Brother Arnold, a novice who was a clerk; and of laymen, Brother Henry of Cologne, Brother Gernot [2]

---

[1] The two dates are 27 October and 11 November.
[2] Boehmer points out that this is the name of a king in the *Nibelungenlied*.

of Worms, and Brother Conrad of Suabia. And they were followed by Brother John of Cologne and Brother Henry of Hildesheim.

41. In the year 1225, Brother Jordan sent lay Brethren throughout Thuringia to find out conditions in the cities. Brother Hermann, the novice priest and preacher, followed them and sometimes preceded them. When he came to Eisenach, where he had formerly been chaplain, and whence he had returned to the Brethren of the German House,[1] he preached often to the people. And by his preaching and the example set by his conversion—in that he had left the great comfort that he had had in the House of the Teutonic Order to humble himself to an Order so lowly and ascetic —the people were no little moved, and the whole city flocked to whatever place he had announced for his preaching. Wherefore the parish priests of the city feared that, if the Brethren clave to one priest, the people would be withdrawn from the other, and one of them offered two churches, and the other, one, to the Brethren, that they might choose which they preferred to abide in. But Brother Hermann did not presume to choose without the Brethren's advice, and asked Brother Jordan to come to Eisenach, bringing a discreet

[1] i.e. the Knights of the Teutonic Order.

companion with him, and to choose, after taking
counsel, what pleased him. And he came, and after
taking counsel, chose the place in which the
Brethren now dwell.[1]

42. In the same year, during Lent, the Brethren
were granted a place in Gotha, in which two
Brethren abode for twenty-five years and generously performed every office of mercy and hos-
pitality, beyond what they could conveniently do,
both for our own Brethren and the Friars Preachers
and all other Religious.

43. In the same year, by the advice of Sir Henry,
parish priest of Saint Bartholomew, and of the lord
Vidame [2] Gunther, and of other burgesses of Erfurt,
the Brethren removed to the church [3] of the Holy
Spirit, that was then standing empty, where formerly some Augustinian nuns had dwelt, and abode
there for fully six years. And when the man who
had been appointed procurator [4] for the Brethren
by the burgesses asked Brother Jordan if he
desired the building to be made like a cloister,
Jordan, never having seen a cloister in the Order,
replied: "I know not what a cloister means: only
build us a house near the water, that we may

---

[1] This was near the Wartburg, the home, after marriage, of
St. Elizabeth.

[2] *Vice domini.*

[3] i.e. the hospital of that name.　　　　[4] Cf. p. 17, note.

go down thither to wash our feet." And so it was done.

44. In the same year, moreover, Brethren were sent to Nordhausen, about the Feast of Saints Peter and Paul. There they were well received by the townsfolk, and were established for their convenience in a garden, for which they paid a rent of three *solidi* yearly. In it there was a house conveniently situated for attending the church. Now the Brethren sent thither were laymen only, and the Custodian became weary of going thither so often as was necessary for hearing their confessions, so, when they had stayed there three years, he recalled them, to their comfort, and established them in other houses. But, in 1230, when a certain maiden gave the Brethren a site, they returned thither.

45. In the same year (1225), at the request of Count Ernest,[1] four lay Brethren were sent to Mühlhausen. He allotted them a new house, without a roof, and the garden adjoining, and, until they should have roofed the house and enclosed the garden, established them in a cellar in the castle. In this the Brethren above mentioned prayed and ate and received guests and slept.

---

[1] Of Velsekke-Gleichen. Boehmer (p. 39, note 3) quotes a romantic story about him.

And because those lay Brethren were satisfied with the cellar and had not been able to roof the house and enclose the garden within a year and a half, the Count saw that there was no profit in them, and began to withdraw his help from them. Thus the Brethren, having no resources wherewith to roof the house and enclose the garden, were driven by necessity to withdraw, and were established in other houses. But in 1231 the Brethren returned thither, and were received in the Hospital by permission of King Henry. But the Master of the Hospital, thinking that whatever was given to the Brethren would be withdrawn from himself, began to be annoying to the Brethren and captious concerning them. This the Brethren could not bear, and, on a certain Knight's giving them a piece of land, they began to build thereon, and still abide there to-day.

46. In the same year, again, the Brethren who had settled outside the walls at Erfurt came into the town.

47. In the same year[1] there was sent from Brother Albert of Pisa, Minister of Germany, to Brother Jordan, then Custodian of Thuringia, to be his comfort and help, Brother Nicholas of the

[1] i.e. 1225, not the 1231 which has just been mentioned in parenthesis.

Rhine,[1] a priest, learned in the law, who is known as Nicholas the humble. Humility pre-eminently shone forth in him. He died at Bologna, having abundant witness to his holiness. When Brother Jordan met him between Gotha and Eisenach, they embraced one another with reverence and in brotherly wise, and thus sat down together. Brother Nicholas was in sooth an humble man, and of a dovelike simplicity, and, as he sat reverently and silently in presence of Brother Jordan, Brother Peter of Eisenach, the companion of Brother Nicholas, himself a mirthful and light-hearted person, who knew the other's humility, said to him: "Brother Nicholas, dost thou not recognise our king and lord?" And he, joining his hands, humbly replied: "Gladly do I know him and I serve my lord." Then Brother Peter added: "See, this is our Custodian." When he heard this, he rose and confessed his fault, with a long apology for having greeted him with such lack of reverence. And, rising, on bended knees with all humility, he presented to Brother Jordan the letters of his mandate. Then Brother Jordan sent him to the house at Erfurt, there to await his behest. And after three weeks Brother Jordan sent him letters

[1] He is so called because he was assigned afterwards to the Custody of the Rhine. See Boehmer, p. 41, note.

appointing him Guardian there. And he received them with reverence, and said: "What hath our father done to me?" Now Brother Jordan was so abashed by the humility of Brother Nicholas that he could scarce endure (to be with) him, and did not venture to go to Erfurt for six weeks. Brother Nicholas, merely by his presence, kept the Brethren in better discipline than any other could by reproofs and precepts.

48. In the same year, Brother James, Custodian of Saxony, founded the church of the Friars Minor in the new city [1] of Magdeburg, and caused it to be consecrated on the Feast of the Exaltation of the Holy Cross [2] by Albert, lord Archbishop of that place. When it was consecrated, the lord Archbishop generously left to the Brethren all the adornment of the altar. And Brother James aforesaid, while he was saying Mass in the Brethren's church on a day within the octave of the dedication, began to feel so weak at its conclusion that he was carried into the Brethren's guest-house, which they then had in the old city near to Saint Peter's. For up to then the Brethren had no buildings in the new city except the church. And there, on the twelfth day before the Kalends

[1] The Neustadt and Altstadt of Magdeburg are alluded to in this section.

[2] 14 September.

of October,[1] that is, on the Vigil of Saint Matthew, he departed unto the Lord. Now the Brethren scarce had a burying-place and had no regular use as to burials, so they consulted together as to what they should do, especially by reason of the Council that was about to be held on the Feast of Saint Maurice, for which many Bishops had already assembled. They decided that they would approach the lord Bishop of Hildesheim, because he honoured Brother James as a father. He had, indeed, given his household orders that, whether he was sleeping, or whether he was doing anything else, if the Brethren wished to speak with him they were to tell him. Now the Bishop was already asleep, but he was awakened, and told that Brother James had died. At this news he wept, greatly moved, and said: "Lo, this is the dream that I have just seen!" And he added: "I will come and bury him." Now in sleep he had seen a dead person clad or wrapped in white, and it had been said to him: "Go and loose him." And the body was brought to the Brethren's church in the new city, which Brother James himself had founded and caused to be dedicated, and there it was buried with honour. But in 1238 his bones, and those of Brother Simon the Englishman (the first

[1] 20 September.

Reader in Magdeburg, and the third Minister), were removed, on the removal of the Brethren to the old city, where they now dwell, and were buried there.

49. Brother James of happy memory being dead, the Brethren of Saxony were no little dismayed, and begged Brother Albert of Pisa, Minister of Germany, to deign of his clemency to provide them with a Custodian. And the Minister proposed to send them as Custodian Brother Nicholas, Guardian at Erfurt. Howbeit, knowing his humility, he did not venture to send him the mandate in writing, fearing that in his humility he would refuse the office, but rather decided that he must be approached in person. Accordingly, he arranged himself to approach him, hoping that in friendly talk he might incline him to take the office. The Minister, then, came to Erfurt and, summoning Brother Jordan on this business, began to speak with Brother Nicholas as to accepting the office of Custodian of Saxony. When that Brother humbly excused himself, and declared himself to be in every way incompetent, saying that one who knew not how to count or reckon could not be a lord or hold high office, the Minister caught him up at that word, and said, as though wroth in spirit: "Thou knowest not then how to be a

lord. Are we therefore lords who hold offices in
the Order? Confess then thy fault quickly, Brother,
for that thou hast thought the offices in the Order,
which may rather be called burdens and servitude,
to be kingdoms and lordships." When he humbly
confessed his fault, the Minister gave him the
Custody of Saxony as his penance, and he, as he
was ever wont, humbly obeyed on bended knee.
And the Brethren greatly rejoiced at the mandate
being given him, and they celebrated it in the
church of the Holy Spirit, where they then abode,
Brother Nicholas singing Mass to the ferial tone[1]
and in a dismal spirit. He, then, being made
the third Custodian of Saxony, did not abandon
his former humility when established in office, but
was always the first and the most humble in
washing the dishes and the Brethren's feet. And if
for some fault he laid a penance on a Brother of
sitting on the ground, or the discipline,[2] he himself,
in his exceeding humility, would perform the same
penance with him. And although he himself maintained humility and obedience in all things, he was
yet such an avenger and punisher of obstinate
disobedience that he could scarce take back into
favour a Brother guilty of that, even when he was

[1] i.e. of plainsong, appointed for days other than great Festivals.
It may mean "funereally."
[2] A small scourge. Cf. Eccleston, p. 36.

penitent. For he considered the disobedience of a Brother so great an evil, and his obedience so great a good, that by deed and example he showed the Brethren how they ought in all things to yield simple obedience.

50. In the year 1226, on the fourth day of October, the first founder of the Order of Friars Minor, our blissful Father Francis, departed to the Lord at Saint Mary of the Little Portion. And albeit our blissful Father, Blessed Francis, desired to be buried in that same church, the people of the district and the citizens of Assisi feared that he might be snatched away by violence by the Perugians, because of the wonders which through him God had deigned to work, in life and after his death. Wherefore they bore him to the church of Saint George[1] near the walls of Assisi—the church in which he had first learnt to read and had afterwards first begun to preach—and there buried him with honour. On the death of Blessed Francis, Brother Elias, his Vicar, sent letters of consolation to the Brethren throughout the Order, who were dismayed at the death of such a Father. He told them one and all, as Blessed Francis had bidden them, that he blessed them all as from Blessed Francis, and absolved them from all sins;

---

[1] Now Santa Chiara.

o

moreover, he gave them news of the Stigmata, and of other marvels which, after his death, the Most High deigned to work by Blessed Francis. Finally, he enjoined on the Ministers and Custodians of the Order that they should come together to elect a Minister General.

51. In 1227, on the second day of the February after the death of Blessed Francis, Brother Albert of Pisa, Minister of Germany, who was about to set forth to the Chapter General for the election of the first Minister General, assembled all the Custodians and preachers and Guardians of Germany and held a Chapter at Mainz. In this Chapter, [Brother Nicholas was released from being Custodian of Saxony, and was made Vicar,[1] and Brother Leonard the Lombard succeeded him. Matters being thus arranged, Brother Albert, together with the Brethren whom he had chosen, set out for the Chapter General. In this Chapter,[2]] Brother John Parenti,[3] a Roman citizen and doctor of laws, a native of Città di Castello,[4] was elected the first [5] Minister General in the Order.

52. He, by the advice of the Minister of France,

[1] Cf. Introduction, p. xxxv.
[2] This whole sentence is supplied by G.; it has dropped out of B.
[3] Cf. Eccleston, p. 77.
[4] This is incorrect. He was born at Carmignano, near Pistoia, but had been a judge at Città di Castello.
[5] Eccleston (p. 77) calls Elias this, but Jordan, more correctly, considers him first Vicar-general, appointed, not elected.

released Brother Albert of Pisa from the administration of Germany, and sent in his place Brother
Simon the Englishman, Custodian of Normandy,
a learned man and a great theologian.

53. Brother Simon, accordingly, came to Germany, together with Brother Julian, who afterward composed the Life of Blessed Francis and of
Blessed Antony in noble style and to a fair melody.[1]
He straightway appointed a Chapter Provincial
to be held in Cologne on the Feast of Saints Simon
and Jude. [But because of some [urgent][2] reason
it was held in the year following.]

54. In the year 1228, Blessed Francis was
canonised. And in the same year Brother Simon,
Minister of Germany, held a Chapter Provincial
in Cologne between Easter and Pentecost. In the
same year, Brother John Parenti, the Minister
General, hearing that there was no Reader in
theology in Germany, released Brother Simon
from being Minister of Germany, and made him
Reader, and appointed Brother John of Piano
Carpine to be Minister of Germany. Brother John
called together a Chapter Provincial at Worms,
where he showed the letters releasing Brother
Simon and appointing himself. And in that same

---

[1] A metrical Office of the two Saints.
[2] A word of some meaning like this has been omitted. The sentence
in brackets is supplied from G.

Chapter the canonisation of Blessed Francis was announced to the Brethren. Then Brother John of Piano Carpine, wishing to honour and exalt Saxony, sent Brother Simon to be the first Reader in Magdeburg, and with him men of worth and probity and learning, Brothers Marquardus the Tall of Aschaffenburg and Marquardus the Short of Mainz, and Conrad of Worms, and many others.

55. This Minister, because he was corpulent, rode on an ass, and the men of that day, by reason of the novelty of the Order, and the lowliness of this rider—who, following the example of Christ, rode an ass rather than a horse—were moved to a greater devotion towards his ass than the men of to-day feel towards the Ministers themselves by reason of their constant association with the Brethren.[1] He was a very great propagator of his Order. For when he was re-elected Minister, he sent Brethren to Bohemia, Hungary, Poland, Dacia, and Norway. He also started a house at Metz and planted the Order in Lorraine. Brother John was likewise a zealous champion of his Order. He made a stand for it, firmly and in person, in the presence of Bishops and Princes. He cherished his Brethren as a mother doth her

---

[1] Reading *propter assiduum fratrum usum*. Boehmer reads [*ab*]*usum* [*equitandi*], supplying the bracketed words from a late text—quite unnecessarily, as Auweiler points out.

sons or a hen her chickens, and ruled over them in peace and love and all consolation.

56. In 1229, Brother John the Englishman was sent to Germany as first Vicar.

57. In 1230, Brother John, Minister of Germany, held his last Chapter Provincial of Germany at Cologne. In this year, after appointing Brother John the Englishman as his Vicar, he set forth for the Chapter General. In this Chapter Brother John of Piano Carpine was released from that office, and was sent to Spain as Minister, and Brother Simon, the first Reader in Germany, was appointed Minister there in his stead. But before the mandate had reached him, his death forestalled it, on the vigil of Blessed Vitus, and he was buried in Magdeburg. In that same Chapter General, the administration of Germany was divided into two parts, one of the Rhine, and one of Saxony. To the Rhine was appointed as Minister Brother Otto, a Lombard learned in the law; to Saxony, Brother Simon, as already told. In that same Chapter General, breviaries and antiphonaries according to the Use of the Order were sent out to the Provinces.

58. On the death of Brother Simon, first Reader and first Minister of Saxony, Brother Leonard, Custodian of Saxony, and Brother Jordan, Custodian of Thuringia, who were the only two

Custodians of the Province of Saxony, went to the Chapter of the Rhine held at Worms. In this Chapter, because there had hitherto been one administration only, and the division was recent, and Brother Simon's death had forestalled his entering on any of the Minister's duties, the matter still remaining as it were intact,[1] they were admitted as Brethren belonging to the body of the Chapter. Here then, by the advice of the Minister and the Vicar and of the other Brethren, Brother Jordan, entrusting his Custody to the Custodian of Saxony, and taking a companion with him, set forth to the Minister General with the mandate of Otto, Minister of the Rhine, to beg for the appointment of a Minister and a Reader. When the Minister General was considering whom he should send, Brother Jordan besought that it might be Brother John the Englishman, formerly Visitor of Germany, and this was granted. So the Minister General wrote to the Minister of France, bidding him send Brother John the Englishman [2] to be Minister of Saxony, and Brother Bartholomew the Englishman to be Reader.

59.[3] Now as Brother Jordan was returning to

[1] Or, "as though the two Provinces were still a single whole."

[2] Cf. chap. 60. It is not explained why Brother John was in Paris when he had been left as Vicar in Germany.

[3] Boehmer (pp. 50–3) gives Glassberger's fuller text of this chapter side by side with that of MS. B. We learn from it that the relics of St. Francis were some of his hair and clothing.

Germany he came to Brother Thomas of Celano, who, rejoicing thereat, gave him some relics of Blessed Francis. And when Brother Jordan reached Würzburg, he told the Brethren of his Custody that, if they had need to speak with him, they should meet him in Eisenach, because he was about to go thither. The Brethren, accordingly, gladly assembled at the place indicated, bidding the porter not admit Brother Jordan when he came, but first inform them. Thus, when Brother Jordan came to the door and knocked he was not admitted, but the porter ran to the Brethren and told them that Brother Jordan was standing at the door. And they bade him again not admit him by the door, but through the church. Then the Brethren, exulting in spirit, entered the choir carrying crosses and a thurible and palm branches and lighted candles in their hand, and, processing two and two, entered the church beyond the choir. And, arranging themselves in a line, they opened the doors of the church, and admitted Brother Jordan, welcoming him with leaping and rejoicing, while they sang the response: "This is he who loves his Brethren." Brother Jordan was amazed at this novel manner of welcome, and beckoned with his hand for silence, but they exultantly finished singing what they had begun. And when

Brother Jordan, quite confounded, was marvelling at this, it came to his mind that he had with him the relics of Blessed Francis, which he had forgotten in his amazement. And, exulting in spirit, as the song came to an end, he said: "Rejoice, Brethren, since I know that it is not myself as such that ye have praised, but through me our Father, Blessed Francis, whose relics I have with me, and who, while I kept silence, kindled your spirits by his presence." And, taking the relics from his bosom, he laid them on the altar. From that time on, Brother Jordan began to hold in greater veneration and honour Blessed Francis, whom he had seen in this present life, by reason of which a certain human view had come to him.[1] For he perceived that God, kindling the hearts of the Brethren by His Holy Spirit, had not allowed the relics in his keeping to remain hidden.

60. In the year 1231, Brother Jordan, Custodian of Thuringia, returned to Saxony, and sent Brother John of Penna with Brother Adeodatus to Paris, that they might bring thence Brother John the Englishman, the Minister, and Brother Bartholomew, the Reader, with all honour into Saxony.

61. In 1232, at the Chapter General held at

[1] i.e. he had regarded him as a mere man.

Rome,[1] Brother John Parenti was released from
the office of Minister General, and Brother Elias
was chosen to succeed him. In the same Chapter
also, Brother John the Englishman, of Reading,
the Minister of Saxony, was released from office,
and Brother John of Piano Carpine appointed in
his stead. Now Brother Leonard, Custodian of
Saxony, had died on his journey back from the
Chapter, in Cremona, his native place, and
Brother Berthold of Hoexter[2] was chosen to
succeed him.

Brother Elias, now made Minister General,
desired to complete the work in connection with
Saint Francis[3] that he had begun in Assisi. Wherefore he made a levy throughout the Order to finish
what had been begun. For he had the whole Order
in his power, just as Blessed Francis and Brother
John Parenti his predecessors had had it. Thus
at his own pleasure he arranged many things that
were ill-suited to the Order. For he held no Chapter
General during seven years, which was contrary
to the Rule, and he scattered the Brethren who
resisted him hither and thither. So the Brethren
held a council, and decided as a community to

---

[1] This is probably a mistake in the MS. Eccleston says Rieti, and,
as Pope Gregory was there at the time, he is probably correct.

[2] In Westphalia.

[3] i.e. the great Church of San Francesco.

see to the welfare of the Order. Foremost among those in this council were Brother Alexander Hales,[1] and Brother John of La Rochelle, who were then Masters in Paris.

62. In 1237, Brother Elias sent to each of the Provinces Visitors to further his schemes.[2] By their irregular Visitations the Brethren were more incensed against him than before.

63. In 1238, the Brethren of Saxony appealed to the Minister General against the Visitor; they sent messengers to him, but gained nothing at all. Whereby they were forced to appeal to the lord Pope. When Brother Jordan came before him, and, having greeted him, was bidden to depart, Brother Jordan did not wish to go forth, but ran joyfully to the couch of the lord Pope and drew forth his bare foot, which he kissed, crying out to his companion: "See, we have no such relics in Saxony!" And as the lord Pope still desired them to leave him, Brother Jordan said: "Nay, lord, we have nought to ask from you now. For through you we abound in all good things, and are proud. For you are the father of the Order, its protector and corrector. But we came only to see you." Then at last the lord

[1] The famous Doctor, and Reader to the Paris Friary. John was his pupil, and successor in that office.
[2] Cf. Eccleston, pp. 54–6.

Pope was moved to mirth, and arose, and sat on the couch, and asked why they had come, adding: "I know that ye have appealed. Brother Elias came to me, and said ye had appealed over his head,[1] and we replied to him that an appeal made to me[2] includes all appeals." Then when Brother Jordan set forth to the Pope the points of the appeal, the Pope answered that the Brethren had done well to appeal. Accordingly, when the different Brethren came together to the Curia, to further the appeal which they had made, a prolonged debate was held, and finally the greater number came to the conclusion that they could do nothing unless they laid their hand to the root, that is, by taking direct action against Elias.

64. And they sat down and made a scrutiny among the Brethren who had assembled, and wrote down all they could know or prove, by act and by report, against Elias. These notes were read out before the Pope, and in his presence debates were held on the question. This disputation the lord Pope quieted by saying: "Go and discuss among yourselves, and write down the objections, and the answers to the objections, and bring them to me, and I will judge." And this was

[1] *Per saltum, lit.* at a bound, i.e. going direct to the Pope.
[2] *Me* (twice) and *nos*, the plural being the usual Papal form.

done. Then the lord Pope, after he had both heard and read the objections and the replies thereto, decreed that the Brethren there assembled should return to their own Provinces, and that twenty discreet[1] Brethren of ripe wisdom should be sent from the different Provinces, and in especial from those which had propounded the question of reform in the Order. These Brethren should meet in Rome four weeks before the Chapter General, and should frame regulations concerning the condition and reformation of the Order.

65. Wherefore, in the year 1239, in accordance with what has been said, discreet Brethren from the different Provinces were sent to Rome, coming by the advice and desire of the lord Pope, and they ordained that the elections of Ministers, Custodians and Guardians should be made by the approval of the Chapter General, and certain other rules which are still observed to-day.[2] Moreover, they decreed that individual Ministers and two elected representatives[3] should hold a Chapter in their Provinces.

66. In the same Chapter, Brother Elias, who had ruled for seven years, was deposed, and Brother Albert of Pisa was chosen in his stead. His election was confirmed by the lord Pope.

[1] For the technical use of the word *discreti*, cf. Introduction, p. xxxiv. [2] Cf. Eccleston, p. 80. [3] *Subditi*. Cf. p. 84, note 2.

67. In the same Chapter, the Provinces were defined.

68. In the same Chapter, Brother John of Piano Carpine, Minister of Saxony, was released from office and Brother Conrad of Worms was chosen in his stead. But he did not accept office because he did not receive his mandate. For when Sister Agnes of Prague[1] heard of it, she sent to the Pope, and in consequence he revoked the appointment of Brother Conrad. In the same year, after the Chapter at Rome, the Brethren of Saxony held a Chapter Provincial at Magdeburg on the Nativity of Blessed Mary the Virgin, and elected Brother Marquardus the Short as Minister. He, as Minister, was a great champion of his Order and of ascetic life. He showed himself kindly to the good and stern to the evil and severe to those that would not be corrected. He suffered from constant ill-health contracted while toiling in the concerns of the Order against Elias. But in spite of it he was elected Minister. By reason of this bodily weakness, he could not set an example of asceticism, and had need to be released himself from the severities he imposed on others. Yet he held three Chapters, before he was released from office, to wit, in Erfurt,

[1] Sister of King Wenzel I. of Bohemia, herself afterwards canonised.

Hildesheim, and Altenburg. At this last he was released.

70. In 1240, on the twenty-third of January, Brother Albert, the third Minister General, died after he had ruled eight months and some days, and was succeeded by Brother Aymon, an Englishman.[1]

71. In 1242, Brother Aymon held a Chapter in Altenburg on the Feast of Saint Michael and at that he released Brother Marquardus from office. This Chapter entrusted the appointment of a Minister Provincial to the Minister General. The Minister General then departed, leaving Brother Jordan as his Vicar, and thus he appointed Brother Gottfried as Minister.

72. In 1243, then, Gottfried entered the Province. He was a man of most temperate habits in eating and drinking, a lover of his community, and a chastiser of eccentricities. He was kindly to the good and stern to the evil. He held on in the way which Brother Marquardus had initiated, and for three years and some months ruled the Province commendably.

73. In 1244, Brother Aymon died, and in the same year Brother Crescentius [2] succeeded him. He summoned to the convent at Rome two

[1] Cf. Eccleston, p. 84.　　　[2] Cf. Eccleston, p. 87.

Brethren from each Province, so that all when they came to the Curia might find Brethren of their own nation with whom to take counsel. But as the Curia made a long stay at Lyons, the Brethren who had been thus sent out were sent back to their Provinces. Now at that time the Brethren were sorely troubled by Frederick, who had been deposed from being Emperor by decree of the Council of Lyons. In many Provinces they were cast forth in confusion from their houses, many of them were arrested, some were even killed — all because, obeying the commands of the Church, they had manfully stood by their holy Mother as her sons, which no other Religious beside the Friars Minor did.

74. At that time Siegfried, Archbishop of Mainz, was troublesome to the Brethren.[1]

75. In the year 1247, Brother Gottfried, Minister of Saxony, who had ruled for three years and some months, was released from office at the Chapter at Lyons, and Brother Conrad of Brunswick, Reader at Hildesheim, was appointed Vicar. And in the same year, at the chapter held at Halle, on the Nativity of Blessed Mary the Virgin, he was elected Minister of Saxony, and his appointment was confirmed about the Feast of Saint

[1] Probably an allusion to his interdict on Erfurt.

Martin. He, in the tranquillity gained for him by his predecessors, ruled the Province with discipline and firmness, in ripe wisdom, and in the observance of the Rule. And when he had ruled for nearly sixteen years, and was worn out by toils and wearied, he obtained his release by great and importunate urgency, to the sorrow of many Brethren.

76. In 1248,[1] at the Chapter of Lyons, Brother Crescentius was released from office, when he and Brother Aymon had ruled for seven years. And in the same year Brother John of Parma was appointed to succeed him.

77. In 1258, at the Chapter held in Rome on the Feast of the Purification [2] (of Our Lady), Brother John of Parma, Minister General, was released from Office, after having ruled for ten years, and Brother Bonaventura, Reader at Paris, was appointed as his successor.

78. In the year 1262, Brother Conrad of Brunswick, Minister of Saxony, was released from office at the Chapter of Halberstadt, and in the same Chapter, on the twenty-ninth day of April, in the first scrutiny, Brother Bartholomew, formerly Minister of Austria, was unanimously chosen to be Minister of Saxony, and the appointment was

---

[1] This should be 1247 (cf. chap. 75).   [2] 2 February.

BROTHER WILLIAM OF ENGLAND
(*See note on page* 190)

confirmed on the spot through Brother Conrad, by the authority of the Minister General. He was elected in his absence and, when summoned, agreed, at the request of the Brethren, to the election of himself, albeit with grief. He presided over that Chapter, and concluded it to the consolation of the Brethren.

The drawing of Brother William, which gives a good idea of the habit, is from a MS. (XVI. f. 67) in Corpus Christi College, Cambridge (A.D. 1236–50), by courteous permission of the Master.

For Brother William, who is not to be identified with William of Nottingham, see A. G. Little, *Collectanea Franciscana*, vol. i. pp. 5–8.

BIBLIOGRAPHY

Among books dealing with the Friars in England, may be mentioned:

COTTON, CHARLES, *The Grey Friars of Canterbury* (British Society of Franciscan Studies, 1924).

CUTHBERT, Father, O.S.F.C., *The Friars, and how they came to England* (Sands, 1903).

—— *The Chronicle of Thomas of Eccleston* (Sands, 1909).

JESSOPP, Dr. A., *The Coming of the Friars* (1889).

KINGSFORD, C. L., *The Grey Friars of London* (British Society of Franciscan Studies, 1915).

LITTLE, A. G., *The Grey Friars in Oxford* (Oxford, 1892).

—— *Studies in English Franciscan History* (Manchester, 1917).

Monumenta Franciscana, Vols. I. and II. (Rolls Series).

SEVER, JOHN, *The English Franciscans under Henry III.* (Blackwell, 1915).

For the history of Elias and the Order:

CUTHBERT, Father, O.S.F.C., *Life of St. Francis of Assisi* (Longmans, Green & Co., 1912).

LEMPP, Dr. E., *Frère Élie de Cortone* (Paris, 1901).

MACDONELL, ANNE, *Sons of Francis* (Dent, 1902).

SABATIER, PAUL, *Speculum Perfectionis*. Attention is called to M. Sabatier's newly revised, definitive edition of this, which is to be published in the present year by the British Society of Franciscan Studies.

INDEX

MADE AT THE
TEMPLE PRESS   LETCHWORTH
IN GREAT BRITAIN

A Descriptive List of Books on
the Life and Teaching of Saint
Francis of Assisi, and of Works
of Franciscan Interest

J. M. DENT & SONS LTD., London

SAINT FRANCIS BOOKS
In the Temple Classics

Saint Francis is represented in this famous series of Classics by four volumes which provide an unrivalled collection of most of the principal authorities for his life and precepts. The four volumes are uniform in format. *They are pocket size, bound in blue cloth with gilt designs on back, top edges gilt, and with red ribbon bookmark. Each has a photogravure frontispiece, designed title-page in red and black, and the volumes are most tastefully printed with wide margins.*

Cloth, 2s. net per volume

THE LITTLE FLOWERS OF SAINT FRANCIS

Specially translated for the series from the Italian *Fioretti di San Francesco* by PROFESSOR SIR T. W. ARNOLD, M.A.

"In this book are found certain little Flowers, Miracles and devout ensamples of the glorious Poor Little One of Christ, Saint Francis, and certain of his holy Companions, to the praise of Jesu Christ."

¶ This edition of the "most exquisite expression of the religious life of the Middle Ages" is a favourite one. First printed in 1898, it is now in its sixteenth edition. A note is included outlining the sources, history and authorship of the *Fioretti*.

THE MIRROR OF PERFECTION

Specially translated for the series from the Cottonian MS. by ROBERT STEELE.

"This book was compiled as a legend from certain ancient ones which the fellows of Blessed Francis wrote and caused to be written in diverse places."

¶ *The Mirror of Perfection—Speculum Perfectionis*—remains the most intimate authority for the last years of the life of St. Francis. It lies at the root of the popular idea of the saint. The photogravure frontispiece is from an unpublished drawing by C. S. Ricketts, "St. Francis and the Wolf of Gubbio."

THE LEGEND OF SAINT FRANCIS BY THE THREE COMPANIONS

Here first translated into English by EMMA GURNEY SALTER.

"These be certain things written by Three Companions of the Blessed Francis concerning his life and his conversation in the worldly state, and of his marvellous and perfect conversion."

¶ A translation of the Latin text of *The Legend of the Three Companions* as it stands in *Sancti Francisci Legenda Trium Sociorum ex. cod. Fulg.* (1898). There is an epilogue by Miss Salter summing up the known facts concerning the work. The frontispiece is from a bas-relief in Sta. Maria degli Angeli, Assisi.

SACRUM COMMERCIUM: THE CONVERSE OF FRANCIS AND HIS SONS WITH HOLY POVERTY

Translated by the REV. CANON RAWNSLEY, with an Introduction by PAUL SABATIER.

¶ This volume gives the original Latin of the *Sacrum Commercium* in addition to the translation by the Rev. Canon Rawnsley, who has also added a chapter on "The Lady Poverty and how St. Francis came to love her." The Latin text was collated with the *Codex Casanatensis* by M. Sabatier, and he also supplied the portrait of St. Francis which forms the frontispiece.

An Edition-de-luxe of
THE LITTLE FLOWERS OF SAINT FRANCIS

Being a translation of *I Fioretti di S. Francesco* by THOMAS OKEY, Professor of Italian at Cambridge University. With thirty plates in full-colour from drawings by EUGENE BURNAND. Royal 4to.

Price £2 12s. 6d.

¶ Since the appearance of Paul Sabatier's *Vie de St. François d'Assise*, the starting-point of the Neo-Franciscan movement, there has been no edition of equal importance and taste. Of this limited edition only very few copies remain.

A SAINT FRANCIS VOLUME
In Everyman's Library

THE LITTLE FLOWERS AND THE LIFE OF SAINT FRANCIS WITH THE MIRROR OF PERFECTION

In one volume, obtainable in three styles of binding. Cloth 2s. net; library binding, 3s. net; leather, 3s. 6d. net.

¶ THE LITTLE FLOWERS has here been translated anew by Thomas Okey, Professor of Italian at Cambridge University, and there is an Introduction by him to the whole volume. The MIRROR OF PERFECTION is in the translation of Robert Steele. The LIFE OF SAINT FRANCIS is a translation by Miss Emma Gurney Salter of the official biography by Saint Bonaventura.

This typical "Everyman's Library" volume contains four hundred pages, giving to the student and reader the utmost possible at a small price. "The three works are printed in the inverse order of their composition, although not of their charm and interest. The *Little Flowers* (*Fioretti*) is a free and amplified Italian translation of a Latin original, *Actus B. Francisci et sociorum ejus*, compiled some time after 1322. The *Mirror of Perfection* (*Speculum Perfectionis*), according to Boehmer, is a compilation, edited by one of the *Spirituali* of the Portiuncula, and based chiefly on documents and memoirs left by Friar Leo, and completed about 1318. Of the date and authorship of the *Life of St. Francis* by St. Bonaventura there is no question. It was written by command of the Chapter-General of Narbonne in 1260, and was intended to be the definite and authoritative Life, and to supersede the great variety of fragmentary Lives then in circulation. Bonaventura went to Assisi for the purpose of consulting documents and to interrogate the surviving companions of St. Francis. . . . So satisfied were the authorities with the result, that at the Chapter-General at Paris in 1266, under the presidency of Bonaventura, it was commanded that the whole of the existing Lives in the friaries of the Order should be destroyed."

THE LITTLE POOR MAN
("IL POVERELLO")

The Life Drama of Saint Francis of Assisi. A Play in Four Acts. By HARRY LEE. Small Crown 8vo. 5s. net.

¶ "One of the most beautiful contributions to Franciscan literature."—ARCHBISHOP HAYES.

THE COMING OF THE FRIARS MINOR TO ENGLAND AND GERMANY

Being the Chronicles of THOMAS of ECCLESTON and JORDAN OF GIANO. Translated by Emma Gurney Salter. With two reproductions of MSS. and three Drawings. Crown 8vo. 5s. net.

¶ Of all the Orders, that of the Grey Friars or Minorites was always by far the most numerous and in many respects the most interesting. Founded by St. Francis in 1209 or 1210, the Friars bound themselves to follow as far as possible the daily public life of Christ —especially His poverty. They came to Germany in 1223, to England in 1224, and made foundations at Canterbury, London, Oxford, etc.; and it is of these early years that Thomas of Eccleston and Jordan of Giano tell.

SAINT ANTHONY OF PADUA

By E. GILLIAT-SMITH. Large Crown 8vo. 6s. net.

¶ Of all the followers of St. Francis, St. Anthony of Padua is the most celebrated; and perhaps more apocryphal stories have been written about him than about any other saint. He was a contemporary of St. Francis, whom he actually met; he entered the Franciscan Order in 1220, four years before the Friars came to England; and he became famous as a preacher, and a teacher of theology, especially at Padua, which town has regarded him as its patron Saint since his canonisation in 1232. Mr. Gilliat-Smith tells the story of his life and work in a style of great simplicity and charm, avoiding the extravagances which are to be found in many of the older chronicles. Imprimatur: F. CARD. BOURNE: *Archiepus. Westmonasterien.*

"To all interested in Franciscan traditions this book will come as a welcome addition to a subject which has ever about it the freshness of a Tuscan spring."—*British Weekly.*

THE STORY OF ASSISI

By LINA DUFF GORDON. Illustrated by NELLY ERICHSEN and HELEN M. JAMES. Fcap. 8vo. 5s. 6d. net.

¶ This volume in Dent's Mediæval Towns Series is necessarily important to the student of Franciscan literature in that it sums up all the data concerning St. Francis and his followers in relation to the town which is inseparable from his name. Of the profuse illustrations in line and half-tone, many are reproductions of famous Franciscan pictures. Folding Maps are included, as well as an Appendix, giving notes of walks for visitors.

SAINT CLARE OF ASSISI:
HER LIFE AND LEGISLATION

By ERNEST GILLIAT-SMITH. Square Demy 8vo. 12s. 6d. net.

¶ In this volume Mr. Gilliat-Smith has gathered together all the available evidence, both of contemporary witnesses and the later mediæval writers, and presents a vivid record of the life and work of St. Clare, the "Little plant of the most blessed father Francis." The book has the "imprimatur" of the Vicar-General of the Arch-diocese of Westminster. The frontispiece is a photogravure reproduction of "The Seraphic Mother," from a fourteenth-century fresco in her church at Assisi.

A SIENESE PAINTER OF THE FRANCISCAN LEGEND

By BERNARD BERENSON. With twenty Reproductions in Collotype. Square Demy 8vo. 7s. 6d. net.

¶ This work offers a critical appreciation of the work of Stefano Sassetta, the Sienese painter of the Franciscan Legend, who, Mr. Berenson judges, "has left us the most adequate rendering of the Franciscan soul that we possess in the entire range of painting." Sassetta's paintings are examined, as works of art and more particularly as expressions of the Franciscan ideal, in comparison with those of Giotto. The reproductions are from pictures by Giotto and his school as well as by Sassetta.

FRANCISCAN LEGENDS IN ITALIAN ART

By EMMA GURNEY SALTER. With twenty Reproductions of Pictures. Large Crown 8vo. 6s. net.

¶ This volume is the first attempt to bring into convenient compass and in English an account of the Franciscan Saints and Legends in Italian art. Mainly it is confined to Italian pictures in Italy, and the location of pictures in churches, etc., is given.